Presented to the Salvation Army
School for Officer Training
Central Territory, In Memory of

COMMISSIONER SAMUEL HEPBURN

THE TEACHING METHODS
OF THE MASTER

The
Teaching Methods
of the Master

By Claude C. Jones, Ph.D.

 THE BETHANY PRESS—St. Louis, Missouri

Preface

Jesus was a teacher of adults. By his skill and the effectiveness of his methods, he proved that the viewpoint and living of grown people can be changed.

Jesus was a teacher of religion. As his field was not that of history or science, we are not to look to him for methods of teaching such subjects.

He is being more and more recognized as the Master Teacher. With seemingly no method, and yet with a skill that made his teaching a model for modern pedagogy and psychology, he set an example which none has equaled. His methods were perfectly adapted to imparting lessons of practical living and ethics.

The aim of this book is to show how the Master taught religion to adults. It is a study of methods rather than of doctrines. Surprisingly little has been written about his teaching methods, but there are many outstanding "lives" of Christ, and many helpful discussions of his teachings.

It is our earnest wish that every Christian teacher may sit at the feet of Jesus and learn of him. Then knowing his methods and filled with his spirit, teach others with increasing effectiveness.

Claude C. Jones

Contents

1.

The Master Teacher's Influence

Jesus Christ was the Master Teacher. From the days when he taught by the sea and in the mountains and in the villages and cities of Palestine until the present, he has been supreme. No other teacher has had such an influence on mankind.

People of his day were enthusiastic about him. John the Baptist called him "the Lamb of God." (John 1:29.) John the apostle spoke of him as "the Word" who was "in the beginning with God." (John 1:1-2.) The apostles applied to him such titles as: "the Messiah" (John 1:41), "the Son of God" (John 1:49), "the Christ, the Son of the living God." (Matt. 16:16.) And one who had been inclined to doubt, finally cried out, "My Lord and my God!" (John 20:28.)

A Samaritan woman decided he was a prophet (John 4:19), and the people of her village declared him to be "the Savior of the world." (John 4:42.)

A ruler of the Jews said, "You are a teacher come from God." (John 3:2.) The temple police declared, "No man

9

ever spoke like this man!" (John 7:46), and the crowds who made up his audiences, including the people in his home town Nazareth, "wondered at the gracious words which proceeded out of his mouth." (Luke 4:22.)

Even the Roman centurion, who stood by the cross, exclaimed, "Truly this man was a son of God!" (Mark 15:39.) His enemies complained "the world has gone after him." (John 12:19.) Children loved him and shouted his praises. (Matt. 21:15.)

History has proved his leadership. Jesus has been supreme through all the centuries. Historians themselves are among his most ardent followers. Hear John S. C. Abbott, an American historian, as he calls Christ the great sovereign. Or Johannes von Müller, Swiss historian, as he declares: "Christ is the key to the history of the world. Not only does all harmonize with the mission of Christ, but all is subordinate to it."

Literature finds in him its highest ideal. Jesus was no writer, yet his teachings are found in 700 languages. Some fifty years ago a bibliography of Jesus Christ was published. The list contained more than 5,000 books in English. No doubt many times this number about the Teacher are in print today in various languages.

There is scarcely any literary character in whose work Jesus does not figure. Samuel T. Coleridge, Matthew Arnold, Ralph Waldo Emerson, General Lew Wallace, and a glorious host sat at the feet of the Christ. Some called him "Lord and Master" and one "the only soul in history who has appreciated the worth of man."

The praises of Charles Lamb are typical of literature's tribute to the Teacher from Galilee. In a company of English writers, Lamb said, "There is only one person I can ever think of after this—If Shakespeare was to come into this room, we should all rise up to meet him; but if that Person was to come into it we should all fall and try to kiss the hem of His garment."

Poetry in all the Christian centuries has honored him. The voices of Robert Browning, Elizabeth Barrett Browning, Sidney Lanier, James Whitcomb Riley, Ella Wheeler Wilcox, Alfred Tennyson, Dante, Shakespeare blend with the voices of others like gifted in a mighty anthem of praise. Shakespeare wrote into his will these words:

I Comend my Soule into the handes of god my Creator hoping & assuredlie beleeving through thonelie Merittes of Jesus Christe my Saviour to be made ptaker of lyfe everlastinge.

Most poets could endorse these words written by John Greenleaf Whittier:

O Lord and Master of us all,
Whate'er our name or sign,
We own Thy sway, we hear Thy call,
We test our lives by Thine.

Art dedicates her masterpieces to Jesus. Under his inspiration the greatest of the artists attain their best. Look upon Correggio's "Ecce Homo," Michelangelo's "Last Judgment," Titian's "Tribute Money," da Vinci's "Last Supper," and Raphael's "The Transfiguration." Add to the list Rembrandt's great tribute in his picture of Jesus blessing the children, or Holman Hunt's painting "The Light of the World." In his divine beauty, Jesus Christ has forever consecrated art.

Music attains her best in hymns, symphonies, and oratorios of praise to Jesus Christ. The greatest of all musicians have

11

found in him their inspiration. And today vast throngs are led in worship by Bach, Wagner, Haydn, Mendelssohn, Beethoven, and other gifted souls. Handel's devotion is voiced in his masterpiece, *The Messiah,* in such words as these: "And He shall reign forever and ever"; "Crown Him Lord of Lords and King of Kings."

Science respects him. This is an age of science and at the same time an age of profound reverence for Jesus Christ. Earlier generations of scientists have joined in this attitude. Copernicus was a faithful Christian. It was Johann Kepler who said, "O God, I am thinking thy thoughts after thee." Galileo professed faith in Christianity and Thomas Huxley acknowledged Christ's hand in history. Sir Oliver J. Lodge expressed belief in the deity of Jesus and Max Müller eulogized the teachings of Christ. In his last years on earth Robert Millikan of California publicly avowed his Christian faith and named many like-minded scientists.

Philosophy has been profoundly influenced by Jesus Christ. He proclaimed no new system of philosophy, yet no one pays him higher tribute than John Stuart Mill, Hegel, or Spinoza. Gotthold Lessing declared him to be "the well-spring of whatever is best and purest in human life." Blaise Pascal says, "Jesus Christ is the center of all, and the goal to which all tends." Though differing widely among themselves, thinkers have united in conceiving that Jesus is the highest personality of philosophy.

Skeptics speak of Jesus in words of highest praise. John Stuart Mill calls him "the guide of humanity," while Renan counts Christ "the perfect model and the greatest among the sons of men." Robert Owen says he is "the irreproachable." Tom Paine, Rousseau, Voltaire pay him tribute and Napoleon names him "the emperor of love." Robert Ingersoll's eulogy of Jesus contains these words: "For that name I have infinite respect and love. To that great and serene man I gladly pay the homage of my admiration and my tears."

The Jewish people admire Jesus greatly. Rabbi Kaufman Kohler declares that he is the highest ideal of the modern Jew. And Rabbi Emil Hirsch says that Jesus is revered by all liberal Jews. Moritz Friedlander, a Jewish author, calls him the world's ideal. Rabbi Henry Berkowitz describes him as the gentlest and noblest Rabbi.

Statesmen acknowledge his supremacy. Washington, Lincoln, Gladstone, Jefferson, Garfield, and Cleveland are representative of a host of such leaders. Daniel Webster's epitaph, written by himself, contains this significant sentence: "My heart has always assured and reassured me that the Gospel of Jesus Christ must be Divine Reality." William McKinley went into eternity with the words of the Lord's Prayer, the prayer Jesus taught his disciples, upon his lips. Queen Victoria always acknowledged Jesus as Lord of lords and King of kings.

All types of mind and men of every temperament and station in society have been inspired by the Master Teacher. Among these we find Peter the impetuous and Matthew the hero of faith, Andrew the fisherman and Nicodemus the ruler. Among his followers in all centuries we find massive intellects, virile souls, great heroes, patient sufferers.

Every age of the world since he taught in Palestine has felt his influence. He is never out of date. His words that met man's needs nineteen centuries ago have retained their value for all succeeding ages.

His influence has been felt among all nations. His Jewish parentage is forgotten as men in all nations claim him as their

Lord and Master. He is the one person at home anywhere in the world. The most primitive and the most highly civilized people claim him.

Great political movements have resulted from men's loyalty to Jesus. We recall the Crusades, the Saxon reformation, the journey of our Pilgrim Fathers to this land of liberty, all because of the name of Jesus.

The moral life of men has been profoundly influenced by the principles Jesus taught. Wherever individuals or nations have even partially adopted his teachings, the character of the people has improved. Foot-binding was stopped in China, cannibalism ceased in parts of Africa, infant sacrifices were discontinued in India.

2.

His Manner of Teaching

In the early part of his ministry, Jesus used declaratory and didactic discourse. None of these discourses seems to have been long, the longest reported being the Sermon on the Mount and his farewell address to his disciples. It is quite probable, however, that no address has been reported in full.

The Master's most effective teaching was by means of a combination of the address and discussion method. While necessarily using the declaratory method before large numbers, in small groups or with single individuals the Master was able to supplement it with didactic dialogue.

His discourses were wholly unlike modern sermons. They lacked a formal unity even though he often quoted Scripture and stressed some great truth.

We may say that Jesus was informal even in his formal discourses. He seemed to have had no method. Being the perfect Teacher he used the highest type of his art, the art that conceals art. But he must have given careful thought to the matter and manner of presentation. The greatest teachers of all time have been those who, like the Master, could use the psychological moment when it came, and use it to teach in such an apparently unstudied way as to make it seem natural.[1]

Jesus spoke authoritatively. It is recorded: "He taught them as one who had authority, and not as the scribes." (Mark 1:22.) What was the difference?

Certainly the scribes possessed authority as those whose task it was to interpret the Law.[2] But they taught by painful analysis, by long-drawn-out reasoning, by quoting the judgments of various rabbis, by a lifeless, deadening, splitting of hairs.

Jesus spoke as one who knew. No theorizing, no uncertainty, no feeble reasoning were his. The ancient seers had spoken with a strong assurance. John the Baptist had spoken boldly. No wonder the people identified Jesus with Isaiah or Jeremiah or some other prophet. They had never heard a man who spoke thus. No wonder "the crowds were astonished at his teaching." (Matt. 7:28.)

Again, his teaching was positive. How often the Master would refer to the negative teaching of the law with its "thou shalt nots," and would add a positive command. The golden rule was known in a negative form among many nations before his time, but he gave it in the positive form.[3]

His language was the language of the people. In this he was true to the pedagogical law that the language used in teaching must be common to teacher and pupil.

---

[1]The informality of Jesus is illustrated in such passages as: Matt. 5:1-2; Mark 4:1; Luke 5:3; John 8:2.

[2]Jesus recognized this authority. See Matt. 23:2-4. Men recognize various kinds of authority. (1) There is the authority of opinion, the opinion of one who has devoted study to a subject. (2) There is the authority of position. The word of doctor, preacher, judge, is often a word of authority. (3) There is an authority of testimony. The testimony of those supposed to know scientific, historical, and geographical matters is respected. (4) There is a place for intuition. Woman's intuition is declared to be more accurate than man's reason. In spiritual matters we call this authority inspiration.

[3]Hume in *The World's Living Religions,* pages 265-267, quotes the golden rule as given in eight systems of religion and philosophy.

16

He cultivated simplicity of expression. This constituted much of the charm and clearness of his lessons. His simple, clear, pointed words were the natural garb of truth and a badge of strength. We are prone to use abstract terms and words that end in "ation" and "ality." Some speak of "the Great First Cause." Nearly everyone talks of Providence. Our Teacher used no such words or expressions, but spoke lovingly and simply of "your heavenly Father" and of "your brethren." He proved that great facts can all be stated in simple language.[4] John W. Wayland says in *Christ as a Teacher,* "For two thousand years the plain, simple words of Jesus of Nazareth have been models for the world—for the truth-seeking and the truth-telling."

The Master was skillful in the art of expressing his thought, never using too many nor too few words. Sometimes he used epigrams.[5] At times his sentences were short and crisp.[6] Sometimes he used rhythmic utterance.[7] He never used tiresome platitudes nor did he deal with unimportant matters.

He was a courageous speaker. We recall the day when his cousin John, a prisoner for the truth's sake, sent some messengers to Jesus. When these men had returned to John, Jesus talked to the multitudes about him, paying him an eloquent tribute. John was Herod's prisoner and soon afterwards was beheaded, yet Jesus dared to praise him before a throng of people.

What was his manner of delivery? It seems that much of the time his speech was characterized by a quiet earnestness. His words showed an intensity of thought. Many times he spoke while seated, following the custom of the times.

His delivery was doubtless unhurried. He was patient in

[4]See Matt. 7:1; 5:17; Mark 2:27.
[5]Matt. 6:34.
[6]Mark 4:24; 8:35; Luke 14:11; 18:14.
[7]Matt. 6:7, 8; 11:17.

dealing with his pupils. We find this deliberate manner before he began the Sermon on the Mount.[8]

We have suggested that usually he was a quiet speaker. This was not always the case. It could not have been so at the feast of tabernacles, for there he stood and cried out his gracious invitation.[9]

He was a sympathetic speaker. His attitude toward the sick and sorrowing would show this quality. His message was one of tenderness, and he attracted to himself all right-minded people. The little children loved him. His own affection for people no doubt explains much of their love for him.

He was not a controversial speaker, though many a time his opponents made it necessary for him to expose their crookedness or correct their wrong ideas.[10] At times, when forced to appear controversial, we find him always frank and candid in his treatment of opponents. Jesus seldom argued. He knew how to deal with people so as to shut off an argument.

He was not a sarcastic speaker, though he was known to use sarcasm.

The Master sometimes spoke with the greatest severity. Always gentle and sympathetic, patient and long-suffering, kind and gracious to the poor, ignorant, weak, or slow of understanding, he turned his heavenly wrath in scathing rebuke upon the covetous, hypocritical leaders of religious and political life.[11] So terrible had become the influence of these hypocrites that Jesus had to denounce them thus to hinder their destructive work.

Jesus who so bitterly denounced hypocrisy is the One who looked with compassion on the multitude and who died that we might live.

---

[8]Matt. 5:1, 2. See also John 7:2-39.
[9]John 7:37-39.
[10]Matt. 23.
[11]Matt. 23:1-39; Luke 16:1-31.

18

3.

His Word Pictures

A religious Teacher with great abstract truths to present and with pupils of varying degrees of knowledge and character, Jesus adopted many means of instruction. In this chapter our attention will be confined to his word pictures.

Though he had read no books on modern pedagogy, Jesus taught with the skill of an educational genius, and in his word pictures he stands out as an artist supreme. Their aptness, range, and results give his pictures a place alone in the history of illustrative teaching.

Jesus knew the wisdom of teaching abstract truth by relating it to the concrete. He sat by a well one day in conversation with a Samaritan woman. In this conversation he used the expressions: "Give me a drink," "Every one who drinks of this water will thirst again, but whoever drinks of the water that I shall give him will never thirst." "The hour is coming when neither on this mountain nor in Jerusalem will you worship the Father."[1] With these concrete terms he was able

[1]For other illustrations see John 4:31-34 where the concrete idea of food is used to teach the abstract truth of obedience to God; Mark 1:17 where concrete fact of catching fish led to the abstract truth of personal work for souls.

to approach the abstract truth of the water of life to quench spiritual thirst.

It would be folly to attempt an exhaustive catalogue of his illustrations that belong in this class. He never told a parable without beginning with the concrete and then teaching the abstract.

A modern teacher who understands this principle will teach courage or honesty or truthfulness by relating stories of persons who have been brave or honest or truthful under difficulties.

A key has always been needed to unlock the door of knowledge. By means of pictures, by the use of a "like," the great Teacher opened the understanding.

Often the comparison was implied. Such unnamed likenesses abound in the Sermon on the Mount.[2]

Sometimes he stated the comparisons. Those who heard and acted upon his words were likened to a wise man who built his house upon the rock; those who heard but did not obey were like a foolish man who built his house upon the sand. He said his generation was like children sitting in the market place.

Sometimes Jesus illustrated truths by means of examples, and so he told stories of the good Samaritan, the rich fool, the rich man and Lazarus, and the Pharisee and the publican.

In the early part of his ministry, Jesus used figures of speech or likenesses or word pictures of extreme simplicity. They were not parables.

Later when he began the use of parables, he at first drew almost every likeness from nature. His illustrations during his later ministry were taken in large measure from man and the struggles of his own soul.

[2]See Matt. 5:13, 14; 7:3, 15, 16, 24-29.

An illustration should be more familiar than the truth to be illuminated. It should lead from the known to the related unknown. In harmony with this law, Jesus took the world as his hearers knew it, the world with its beauty and ugliness, its joys and its trials, its play and its work, and used it to show them spiritual truths to which they had been blind.

The mental pictures of the great Teacher give us a panoramic view of life in Palestine.

There are views of organic life. He spoke of salt, light, bread, vines, lilies, the wind, the glowing sunset with its promise of fair weather, the red of the morning with its suggestion of approaching storm, the lightning from the east.

There are pictures of living creatures. We hear the birds singing or we find them building their nests or lodging in the branches of the mustard tree. Now we see a sparrow lying dead on the ground, and again the eagles and the carcasses. Foxes are in their holes and wolves are watching for the sheep, while doves are going on their harmless course. Dogs are under the table, or at the gate licking the sores of a poor beggar. An ox has fallen into a well or a sheep into a pit, and there is the suggestion of a camel trying to go through a needle's eye. Wolves are seen trying to appear as sheep.

We have many glimpses of industrial life. We see the log of wood and splinters. We see food being preserved with salt, or salt that lost its taste being used for roads, used to be trodden under men's feet. The sower goes forth to sow his seed, and an enemy secretly sows weeds and makes the farmer's problem great. Then there is the fig tree with its ripe fruit and the fruitless tree, green with leaves; the mustard seed with its marvelous growth; the grape vines full of luscious grapes; the fading grass; the slow-growing grain; and fields of grain white for the harvest. Herds of swine are feeding. Fishermen are using their dragnets and separating the good

21

from the bad, casting away the worthless ones. Other men are toiling all night, using their cast nets. Still others sit in the boat mending a broken net. A farmer discovers a buried treasure, or a merchant's search for pearls is rewarded by the finding of a most valuable jewel. We see a great millstone and can imagine the mill in operation. We have a glimpse of the successful farmer who builds greater barns and feels secure for the future. Then there is the tragic picture of the men out of work, waiting at the "employment bureau" for a call. The dissatisfaction with the wages and the complaint are described. A debtor is sent to prison and another falls down before his employer and pleads for time. A man is scourged for some misdeed. A thief tries to steal sheep. We see the land-tenants who would not fulfill their contract with the owner. We find industry with its corruption carried on even in the temple court.

There are pictures of the social customs of the day, references to appropriate garments to be worn at a wedding, the arrangement of seats at a feast according to one's social position, the custom of inviting guests who could reciprocate instead of inviting the needy, the closing of doors at the marriage feast and refusal of admittance to late arrivals.

The home life is pictured. Children come to Jesus and he speaks lovingly of them. A woman at home is searching for a valued coin, and her neighbors are called in to share her joy at finding it. A doctor is called in to minister to the sick. A brokenhearted father, a self-satisfied boy, and a prodigal are in one home. Jesus pictured a house on the rock, another on the sand, and then the storms that test the two foundations. The children of the home are playing their games in the market place. They play a game of wedding or funeral. They come home hungry and are sure that father

22

will give them bread and fish. In the broken home, the widow is seeking justice at a corrupt court. A mother is kneading her dough, or the family sits about the table with the dogs at their feet. The lamp is on the stand giving light throughout the house. Again at a late hour, all members of the family are in bed, and a neighbor knocks on the door. Late company has arrived and there isn't enough food in the house. We see a disobliging man who grumbles as he finally gets up to grant his neighbor's request.

Jesus used illustrations that were easily understood by his hearers. Often the references were to the everyday experiences or the native interest of the people. How readily would women respond to the story of a woman kneading dough or searching frantically for the lost coin received perhaps in connection with her marriage! How fascinating to a farmer would be the stories of seed sowing, rich harvests, vineyards pruned rigorously, then in due time bearing luscious fruit! How easily they grasped the truth about weeds growing with the wheat and being hard to eradicate! And the shepherds, or the multitudes familiar with shepherd life, how they would revel in the story of sheep that were safe! Their sympathy would go out to the shepherd away on the mountains in search of the sheep that was lost. The fisherman Simon heard him say, "Henceforth you will be catching men." But these words were not spoken until an interesting thing had been brought to pass. Simon had fished all night and caught nothing. Jesus said, "Let down your nets for a catch." Peter and the others obeyed with the result that "they enclosed a great shoal of fish." This added great significance to the promise that Peter should become one who would catch men.

It is evident that Jesus did more than use familiar things as illustrations. He knew the art of using familiar things freshly. Having eyes with which to see their undiscovered meanings, he brought out their hidden significance.

The word pictures of the Teacher were never so unique, unreasonable, or fascinating as to obscure the truth they were to illustrate. They were not incongruous or suggestive, for Jesus knew that indirect suggestion is usually preferable to direct suggestion.

4.

His Use of Figures of Speech

We have already found that the speech of Jesus abounded in imagery. He seemed to think in pictures.

He used comparisons as his principal method of making truth intelligible. He showed how exacting is discipleship by references to the cost of building a tower and the importance of a king considering the strength of his army before engaging in a war.[1]

Even when sounding out warnings Jesus was still the artist, with beauty of phrase and clearness of thought, for example, in his parable about chief seats and his warning: "When you are invited by any one to a marriage feast, do not sit down in a place of honor, lest a more eminent man than you be invited by him." (Luke 14:8.)

Jesus used many comparisons when he would reprove or exhort. In the Sermon on the Mount he said, "The eye is the lamp of the body. So, if your eye is sound, your whole body will be full of light; but if your eye is not sound, your

---

[1]For some examples of this see: Matt. 10:16; 13:52; 23:26; 23:27; 24:27; 25:32; Luke 13:34.

whole body will be full of darkness. If then the light in you is darkness, how great is the darkness!" (Matt. 6:22-23.) At another time he likened his generation to children at play. Several of the parables in Matthew, chapter 13, contain warnings in the form of comparisons.

The Teacher liked the play upon words. At the time Peter made the Good Confession, Jesus said, "You are Peter (Petros, rock), and on this rock (petra) I will build my church." (Matt. 16:18.)

Jesus often used with a figurative meaning words which in themselves would suggest only the commonplace. He used "water" and "well" figuratively in his conversation with the woman of Samaria. This spiritual water springs up unto eternal life. He used "manna" and "bread" to suggest vital spiritual meanings. He called the Pharisees "offspring of vipers," with the very apparent meaning that they were bad, poisonous. He used "eye" figuratively when, in his greatest sermon, he said, "The eye is the lamp of the body. So, if your eye is sound, your whole body will be full of light; but if your eye is not sound, your whole body will be full of darkness!" (Matt. 6:22-23.)

The great Teacher used practically every figure of speech known today. It is not necessary that we catalogue all of his sayings but it will be instructive and helpful for us to name the figures and give an illustration or two of his use of each.[2]

Simile. This is the simplest way of saying that one thing is like another. Example: "You are like whitewashed tombs." (Matt. 23:27.) Jesus used the simile to associate the objects and experiences of everyday life with his teachings.

Metaphor. In a metaphor a thing or act is either named or implied when another is meant. It is a simile with "like"

[2]For further discussion of this subject, see *Jesus—the Master Teacher,* by Herman Harrell Horne, Chapter XVIII.

omitted. Example: "Go rather to the lost sheep of the house of Israel." (Matt. 10:6.) By means of such effective metaphors as this and others like his figures of bread, salt, light, and leaven, Jesus showed himself a master of metaphor.

Hyperbole. The hyperbole is a rhetorical overstatement of some characteristic or quality. In the nature of the case, its effect is quite often humorous. Example: "You blind guides, straining out a gnat and swallowing a camel!" (Matt. 23:24.)

Epigram. An epigram is a brief contrast that states the opposite of what one would expect. Example: "The last will be first, and the first last." (Matt. 20:16.)

Paradox. A paradox is a statement contrary to accepted opinion. Jesus often helped his hearers think by the seeming contradiction in his utterances. Example: "Every one who exalts himself will be humbled, and he who humbles himself will be exalted." (Luke 14:11.) His use of the paradox has been likened to the shaking of the pupil's shoulder to arouse him from intellectual slumber.

Irony. In irony the speaker means the opposite of what he says. Jesus seldom used it, and even then his words were generally tempered by humor. When he spoke of the Pharisees as those "righteous persons who need no repentance," or when he said of the critical scribes and Pharisees, "Those who are well have no need of a physician, but those who are sick" (Luke 5:31), he used irony.

Metonymy. Metonymy takes the accompaniment of the idea that serves the purpose at the time, naming the idea by this accompaniment and ignoring the rest. Example: "I must preach the good news of the kingdom of God to the other cities also." (Luke 4:43.) By other cities he means the people in the other cities.

27

Synecdoche. Synecdoche consists in taking just the part of the idea that serves the present purpose and letting the part represent the whole. Example: "I have food to eat of which you do not know." (John 4:32.)

Antithesis. Antithesis is the contrast of one idea with another. Jesus used this principle of contrast in various ways and with uniformly strong effect. Example: "If any one would be first, he must be last of all and servant of all." (Mark 9:35.) He contrasted individuals: the Pharisee and the publican, two sons when told to work, three men in the parable of the good Samaritan, the rich man and Lazarus, the two groups at the judgment, and the wise and foolish virgins. The Sermon on the Mount abounded in striking contrasts. In contrast each idea or person is given prominence, interest is quickened, there is a great appeal to the imagination, and therefore teaching is made more effective.

Climax. Climax is derived from a Greek word which means "ladder," an upward progress, with interest and vigor increasing. Example: In his account of the judgment, Jesus draws a vivid picture of the king and the people as those on the right hand are addressed. "Come, O blessed of my Father, inherit the kingdom prepared for you from the foundation of the world." (Matt. 25:34.) And those on the left hand hear the command, "Depart from me, you cursed, into the eternal fire prepared for the devil and his angels." (Matt. 25:41.) Jesus reached his climax in the words, "They will go away into eternal punishment, but the righteous into eternal life." (Matt. 25:46.)

Exclamation. Exclamation suggests active feeling. Example: In Matthew, chapter 23, Jesus is reported to have seven times used the same exclamation: "Woe unto you, scribes and Pharisees, hypocrites!"

Apostrophe. In giving one definition of apostrophe we say it is a figure of speech by which a speaker turns from his audience and addresses just one person. This was done by Jesus when he turned from his apostles, to whom he was speaking, and addressed Peter alone: "Simon, Simon, behold, Satan demanded to have you, that he might sift you like wheat, but I have prayed for you that your faith may not fail; and when you have turned again, strengthen your brethren." (Luke 22:31-32.)

But apostrophe has a wider meaning. In this wider sense the absent, or the dead, or even inanimate things are addressed as if present and able to hear. Jesus used apostrophe when he cried, "Woe to you, Chorazin! woe to you, Bethsaida! for if the mighty works done in you had been done in Tyre and Sidon, they would have repented long ago in sackcloth and ashes. But I tell you, it shall be more tolerable on the day of judgment for Tyre and Sidon than for you." (Matt. 11:21-22.) He also used apostrophe when he addressed Capernaum: "And you, Capernaum, will you be exalted to heaven? You shall be brought down to Hades. For if the mighty works done in you had been done in Sodom, it would have remained until this day. But I tell you that it shall be more tolerable on the day of judgment for the land of Sodom than for you." (Matt. 11:23-24.)

Allusion. This is a hint, or a reference to something not directly mentioned. When the Jews asked Jesus for a sign, he replied, "Destroy this temple, and in three days I will raise it up." (John 2:19.) He was alluding to the temple of his body.

Interrogation. When interrogation is used as a figure of speech, the question is asked, not for an answer, but to imply that the opposite is true. It is a challenge. Jesus was skillful at interrogation, and sometimes he settled the matter by a single question. Example: In the parable of the householder, the laborers murmured about their wages, though each received the wages promised him. The householder said, "Friend, I am doing you no wrong; did you not agree with me for a denarius?" (Matt. 20:13.) Then the employer settled the dispute with the interrogation, "Am I not allowed to do what I choose with what belongs to me? Or do you begrudge my generosity?" (Matt. 20:16.)

Parable. The shortest definition of a parable is that it is a lengthened simile. After the first period of his ministry, this became the most characteristic form of speech Jesus used. We have allotted a whole chapter to this subject. The parables of Jesus are recorded in the Gospels written by Matthew, Mark, and Luke.

Allegory. An allegory is a lengthened metaphor. In it the symbol and the thing symbolized are absolutely identified. An allegory, unlike a parable, does not need an interpretation brought from without itself. The allegories of Jesus are recorded only in the Gospel of John. In John 10:1-10 is recorded the allegory of the sheepfold. In it Jesus teaches the saving power of truth. He declares, "I am the door." In the same chapter is recorded the allegory of the good shepherd. He says, "I am the good shepherd." He taught by this means that he was the way and the life giver and that his love extended beyond them to other sheep. In chapter 15, John recorded the allegory of the vine and the branches. Jesus declared, "I am the vine, you are the branches." The Master stresses the vital relations that exist between the Father and Jesus and the disciples. Each needs the other. In John 11:25-26, Jesus said, "I am the resurrection and the life; he who believes in me, though he die, yet shall he live, and whoever lives and believes in me shall never die." When the words of this metaphor are considered with the conversation of which his statement was a part, they become part of an allegory that draws parallels between Jesus and the resurrection, and between Jesus and life.

Near the end of a helpful chapter on the imagery of Jesus, Horne says,

> The New Testament rewritten without imagery would be less subject to misunderstanding, but it would be stale and flat, even if such rewriting were possible. Try to state the meaning without imagery of "Ye are the salt of the earth . . . ye are the light of the world." Such an effort reveals how Jesus saved words, packed words with meaning, feathered them with imagery, and set them flying on the winds of the world.[3]

[3]From *Jesus—the Master Teacher,* by Herman Harrell Horne. Copyright, Association Press. Used by permission.

5.

His Use of Parables

In his parables, Jesus showed himself a master of the art of storytelling. He showed a grasp of every principle known to modern teachers.

His parables are marvels of unity and condensation. We find not one exception to this statement, but for illustration we may analyze the parable of the rich fool. (Luke 12:16-21.) In the five short verses that tell the story we are introduced to a rich man and to ground that brought forth plentifully. The direct discourse is used as the man addressed himself and as God addressed him. There is suggestion of action throughout the parable. The moral is in the story and there is a climax. The parable is very brief, yet the addition or subtraction of a word would weaken it. Jesus' language was always so concise and pointed "as to stick in the memory like an arrow."

Each parable appeals to the imagination. They possess a rare simplicity and beauty. What could be briefer, more beautiful, more imaginative, than the short parable of the pearl of great price? "The Kingdom of the Heavens is like a jewel merchant who is in quest of choice pearls. He finds one most costly pearl; he goes away, and though it costs all he has, he buys it."[1]

In his parables, Jesus followed with faithfulness and skill what is known today as the educational law: from the concrete to the abstract; from the simple to the complex; from things through symbols to relations. We find the Master telling stories based on the things familiar in the daily lives of his hearers, on things animate and inanimate, on animals, and on the possible experiences of people.

The Gospels record eight parables of the kingdom,[2] nearly all of which are drawn from nature. But when all of his parables are examined, it will be found that his chief interest was in the human world.

We have sixteen parables of the second period of the Master's ministry, in all of which the comparisons are borrowed from man himself.[3]

He used direct discourse. For illustration we will refer to the parable of the unrighteous steward. The rich man of the story addressed the steward. The steward reasoned to himself, then he addressed each one of his lord's debtors, and they answered him, and in every case direct discourse in the parable was the closing statement: "The master commended the dishonest steward for his prudence; for the sons of this world are wiser in their own generation than the sons of light." (Luke 16:8.)

[1]Matt. 13:45-46, *The New Testament in Modern Speech* by Richard Francis Weymouth.

[2]They are: the sower, the wheat and the tares, the grain of mustard, the secret growth of the seed, the leaven, the hid treasure, the pearl of great price, and the dragnet.

[3]They are: the two debtors, the two insolvent debtors, the good Samaritan, the three loaves, the rich man's meditation, the watching householder, the barren fig tree, the marriage supper, the lost sheep, the lost piece of silver, the prodigal son, the unrighteous steward, the rich man and Lazarus, the importunate widow, the Pharisee and the publican, and the laborers in the vineyard.

A study of each parable will show that the stories of Jesus were full of action rather than description and that they were always interesting, adapted to the audience, and invariably true to life. An authority on the art of storytelling says: "The stories of the Gospels have done infinitely more to influence the lives of men than all the books of systematic theology that the Church has produced in twenty centuries of time."[4]

So far in this chapter our discussion has been confined to the story method of teaching spiritual truth. Some parables told by Jesus were in story form and some of his stories were allegories rather than parables. It becomes necessary, therefore, to define a parable.

A parable is a fictitious statement to illustrate familiar things or events true to life from which spiritual facts may be concluded.

The words "proverb" and "parable" represent one Hebrew word māshāl and are used interchangeably in certain passages of the Greek New Testament, yet they are different forms of teaching. For example: "Physician, heal yourself" is a proverb (Luke 4:23), though here it is termed a parable. In Luke 5:36 we read: He told them a parable also: "No one tears a piece from a new garment and puts it upon an old garment; if he does, he will tear the new, and the piece from the new will not match the old." This may also be called a "parable germ." It is really a brief parable undeveloped.

Parable germs are clear statements of customs or happenings and readily bring to mind some religious truth. Consider this one: "If a blind man leads a blind man, both will fall into a pit." (Matt. 15:14.) Here is an event that might

<hr>

[4]From *Stories and Story-Telling*, by Edward Porter St. John, page 3.

easily occur, the moral is apparent, but a story has not been worked out.

The true form of a parable is the story form worked out in such a way as to make a statement of one thing with another meaning back of it. Read the parable of the sower. This parable speaks of the sower, seeds, wayside, rocky places, thorns, good ground, and really means the word of the kingdom and different sorts of hearers.

Some parables are primarily illustrations and are different in form from (1) the short, pointed comparison or (2) the story that states one thing and means another. This third sort of parable may embody in itself the whole truth to be taught and in the same realm. This is the case with the parables of the good Samaritan, the rich fool, the rich man and Lazarus, and the Pharisee and the publican.

A parable is not an allegory, though the two closely resemble each other. The parable suggests the figurative form and the allegory hides it. The parable needs an interpretation for the truth to be grasped, while an allegory proceeds side by side with, or near, the interpretation. The allegory identifies what is represented with the symbol itself. The difference between the two has been illustrated by Richard Trench. He says "Behold, the Lamb of God!" is an allegorical expression, for Christ is identified with the Lamb, but Isaiah's expression, "Brought as a lamb to the slaughter" is parabolic because there is no identification but simply a comparison.[5]

A parable is very different from a fable. Fables move on a lower plane and are generally concerned with ridiculous conversations and deeds of animals. On the other hand, the parables of Jesus are on a lofty plane dealing with events that might occur without transcending reason or nature.

[5]See *Notes on the Parables of Our Lord.*

35

A parable is not a myth. The myth presents itself as the truth, whereas the parable carefully draws a distinction between its form and the truth it illustrates.

Jesus found the parables well suited to the limited mental and spiritual development of his hearers. They aroused interest and caused reflection. To the disciples whose reflection caused a desire for more light, he gave clear expositions of the parables.

We must inquire further into the Master's reasons for the use of this method. When his disciples asked, "Why do you speak to them in parables?" (Matt. 13:10), he gave what might at first seem a peculiar reason: "To you it has been given to know the secrets of the kingdom of heaven, but to them it has not been given." (Matt. 13:11.) Some readers are mystified by this answer because of the impression that the parable was an illustration that made truth clearer. This is the case with some of his parables. These were told simply to enable his hearers to grasp his meaning. But the parable had another purpose as well, and it is this purpose that Jesus states in answering the inquiry of the disciples. He closed his first parable with the words: "He who has ears, let him hear." (Matt. 13:9.) To the spiritually minded, the truth would be made clear. The disciples were "to know the secrets of the kingdom of heaven" (Matt. 13:11), but not so these people, for "seeing they do not see, and hearing they do not hear, nor do they understand." (Matt. 13:13.) They fulfilled Isaiah's prophecy because their hearts were wrong. Jesus uttered spiritual truths in such a way as to enlighten the spiritually minded. He followed his own instructions to keep sacred things sacred. His words will be recalled: "Do not give dogs what is holy; and do not throw your pearls before swine, lest they trample them underfoot and turn to attack you." (Matt. 7:6.)

Often the parable was obscure but caused reflection. To the little group who desired to know the meaning of the first parable, he explained it in detail. After telling several other parables, the Teacher asked, " 'Have you understood all this?' They said to him, 'Yes.' " (Matt. 13:51.) The disciples found it difficult to get the spiritual viewpoint. After another lesson, Peter said to him, "Explain the parable to us." (Matt. 15:15.) Jesus was disappointed at their spiritual dullness, for he said, "Are you also still without understanding?" (Matt. 15:16.) But on this occasion as on many others, the Teacher patiently unfolded the truth to his pupils.

His parables had a meaning beyond the literal statements. The hearer could not be passive if he would get the meaning. Neither could he be simply receptive. The spiritual value was to be found only by the exertion of one's own powers of reflection and interpretation. John W. Wayland states the purpose of parables in these beautiful and clear words: "We see that while parables are illustrations, and in so far are windows admitting light into the temple of truth, they are at the same time windows with curtains. A curtain allows enough light to enter for those inside to see, but it also prevents the curious throng outside from gazing in. The way to have the benefit of the window and the curtain too is to come inside the house. The Great Teacher was continually inviting the multitudes to come inside. Inside all was displayed to view. He never failed to explain a parable, fully and sympathetically, when one came inside and desired to know."[6]

The use of the parable was indirect teaching. Direct teaching states the facts. Indirect teaching leads the pupil

[6]From *Christ as a Teacher*, pp. 27-28. Used by permission of the author.

to find truth for himself. What better example of effective instruction can be found than the parable of the good Samaritan?

Parables are a great aid to the memory. We of modern times know the comparative ease with which stories are recalled long after they are heard; and we know how often direct instruction has been forgotten. We are not surprised then to find that the Gospel writers recalled so many of the Master's story sermons that about one third of their writings consist of these parables. We of today recall his parabolic teaching more readily than his other instruction.

Each parable was told to teach one central truth. The point may be in the entire scene, but often it is in just one aspect. The details are necessary for the completion of the story, but beyond the truth intended no explanation may be needed. In the parable of the good Samaritan, the truth illustrated was neighborliness. It would do violence to the parable to try to make each character and perhaps even the animal and the inn and the money have special designations.

6.

His Use of Objects

The great Teacher used many objects in teaching the mysteries of the kingdom.

To the Samaritan woman who came to draw water, he put the request, "Give me a drink." With water from this well as the starting point, he began an interesting conversation that led to the lesson about the living water, and to the statement of the truth that God is a Spirit, and to the revelation that Jesus is the Christ.[1]

To a ruler of the Jews, with whom he was discussing the new birth, the Master referred to the wind as an illustration.[2] It is interesting to note that he adopted the same method in instructing a learned ruler of the Jews as in teaching a Samaritan woman.

Some Pharisees and Herodians came to him with a catch question. "Is it lawful to pay taxes to Caesar, or not? Should we pay them, or should we not?" They knew that in the divided state of the Jews, his answer might embarrass

---

[1]See John 4:1-26.
[2]See John 3:1-14.

his work. What did he do? He gave an object lesson. He even made the hypocrites provide the object. "Bring me a coin," said he, "and let me look at it." Then he put to them a pointed question, "Whose likeness and inscription is this?" His answer, all the answer to which they were entitled, then came like a shot: "Render to Caesar the things that are Caesar's, and to God the things that are God's." (Mark 12:14-17.)

Jesus took his chosen disciples to the region of Caesarea Philippi. Here among the rocks of this country, he asked his followers, "Who do men say that the Son of man is?" Then a little later, "He said to them, 'But who do you say that I am?' Simon Peter replied, 'You are the Christ, the Son of the living God.'" When Peter had thus made the good confession, "Jesus answered him, 'Blessed are you, Simon Bar-Jona! For flesh and blood has not revealed this to you, but my Father who is in heaven. And I tell you, you are Peter, and on this rock I will build my church, and the powers of death shall not prevail against it' (Matt. 16: 13-18)." The Greek for "Peter" is *petros,* for "rock" it is *petra.* Here the objects lay before them for the lesson on the rocklike character to be attained by Simon and the stability of the church to be built on the firm foundation: Jesus, the Christ, the Son of the living God.

We can readily believe that when the Teacher spoke of lilies, they were growing near by; when he referred to birds or trees or the vine and branches, they were in clear view of the people. We are certain that when he talked of fishers of men, he was in a boat with fishermen whose net had just been full of fishes of the sea.[3] It is easy to imagine a sower at his planting when Jesus told the parable of the sower.

---

[3]See Luke 5:3-11.

He also made use of symbols in the form of acts. Religious symbols are object lessons, no matter what may be their purpose. Baptism symbolizes the new life, and was thus associated with moral regeneration. Jesus himself submitted to it, saying to John, "Thus it is fitting for us to fulfil all righteousness." (Matt. 3:15.) The Great Commission includes it.

The Lord's Supper, partaken of by the disciples, is used as a symbol of their Leader's broken body and shed blood. This symbol keeps alive their remembrance of this proof of his love.

Jesus washed the disciples' feet, a symbol of the humble service one should render another.

The child was used as a symbol of qualities people should possess for entrance into the kingdom. Children were perhaps his best object lessons, his "masterpiece illustration."

When sent forth on a special mission the twelve were told, when a city would not receive them, to "shake off the dust that is on your feet for a testimony against them." (Mark 6:11.) This symbol was a testimony.

Jesus used the symbol of the cross to indicate the sacrifice necessary to be his disciple. "If any man would come after me, let him deny himself and take up his cross and follow me." (Mark 8:34.)

The great Teacher often used adults as object lessons. Many times questions were asked of him, and he, in turn, would use the questioner as an object lesson. For such illustrations we refer the reader to our chapter, "His Questions and Answers."

Adults were used at many other times. A man made this request, "Teacher, bid my brother divide the inheritance

41

with me." (Luke 12:13.) This man with his petition became the object of a lesson on what life really consists. Jesus gave a warning against covetousness and added, "A man's life does not consist in the abundance of his possessions." (Luke 12:15.) This he illustrated by the parable of the rich fool, closing with the remark: "So is he who lays up treasure for himself, and is not rich toward God." (Luke 12:21.)

The Teacher was a guest in a Pharisee's home. The courtesy of washing the feet, of anointing the head with oil, or giving a kiss of welcome had been neglected by the host. A sinful woman entered, wept over Jesus and wet his feet with her tears. She wiped his feet with the hair of her head, kissed them, and anointed them with precious ointment. Jesus addressed his host, showing the true hospitality of this woman. Then to the woman he spoke words of peace.[4]

The Master himself was an object lesson. The chosen twelve were the constant companions of Jesus, hearing his messages to the multitude and to small groups, receiving personal instruction, seeing the mighty works he performed, and even seeing him in prayer, or hearing his words spoken to the Father. How natural for them to ask, "Lord, teach us to pray." Jesus taught his disciples to do things by letting them see him do similar acts. His deeds of healing were evidences of his divine power, but they were also of great teaching value, because Jesus accompanied them by words of instruction. John's Gospel bears particular witness to this feature of his work.

Often he was dramatic in his manner of teaching. He taught by action. His use of word pictures and inanimate objects were supplemented by his own deeds. He gave an

---

[4]Luke 7:36-50.

object lesson on service and humility when he washed the disciples' feet. He had dramatized his statements, such as, "I am among you as one who serves" (Luke 22:27) or this, "I am gentle and lowly in heart." (Matt. 11:29.)

His feeding of the five thousand, and later, of the four thousand, were effective dramatizations of the teaching that Jesus is the bread of life. Though we believe his primary purpose was to meet the physical needs of the hungry people because he had compassion on them, yet we cannot fail to recognize the didactic aspect of the miracles.

Was not his triumphal entry into Jerusalem, as he rode upon a colt, the foal of an ass, the dramatizing of his Messiahship? The people were expecting a king and many were wondering if he were the One of whom the prophets had spoken.

There were two occasions on which Jesus cleansed the temple. In both he was intensely sincere and impressively dramatic. These dramatic acts definitely reinforce his lessons of trust and prayer and reverence.

John the Baptist sent his disciples to ask Jesus, "Are you he who is to come, or shall we look for another?" Then the writer tells what Jesus did: "In that hour he cured many of diseases and plagues and evil spirits; and on many that were blind he bestowed sight." This answer was dramatic. Then came the verbal answer: "Go and tell John what you have seen and heard: the blind receive their sight, the lame walk, lepers are cleansed, and the deaf hear, the dead are raised up, the poor have good news preached to them. And blessed is he who takes no offense at me." (Luke 7:18-23.) This was sufficient answer.

Jesus was an object lesson even in his silences. On the night in which Jesus was betrayed, Simon three times denied his Lord. Then it was that the cock crowed, "and the Lord

43

turned and looked at Peter" (Luke 22:61). No word spoken, but who doubts that Peter remembered that look to the last day of his life? Jesus looked, and "Peter remembered the word of the Lord, how he had said to him, 'Before the cock crows today, you will deny me three times.' And he went out and wept bitterly." (Luke 22:61-62.)[5]

His character was the best object lesson the Teacher put before his pupils. All that he taught in words, he exemplified in conduct. He lived his principles of life. Had he never spoken of courtesy, democracy, diligence, of duty to parents, of friendship, of Scripture study, of the privilege and necessity of prayer, of obligations to God and man, of love to our Father and to human beings as manifested in every experience of life, his own conduct would have impressed these facts upon all who knew him. Each of us has memories of men and women who have taught us in church and in school. How dim the memory of the facts taught compared to the vivid pictures we have of the teachers! The teacher is more than the lesson. Jesus the Teacher Supreme lived his own message.

---

[5]For other accounts of the silence of Jesus see: John 8:6; Matt. 26:63; 27:12-14; Mark 15:4, 5; Luke 23:9; John 19:9.

7.

His Use of Questions and Answers

The teaching skill of the great Teacher seems to have reached its best in the art of questioning. The Gospels are filled with his questions and with those provoked from others because of them and of his lessons associated with them.

His first recorded words as a boy of twelve were a question addressed to his mother, "How is it that you sought me? Did you not know that I must be in my Father's house?" (Luke 2:49.) This was thought-provoking, and like his questions in later life, opened the way to spiritual truth.

He began his choice of disciples with a question. "What do you seek?" The question gave the two courage to make an inquiry of him. The result at that time was: "They stayed with him that day."

Before proceeding further it will profit us to compare his general method with that of Socrates after whom the question-and-answer method of teaching is called the Socratic method. Socrates used what is termed "a leading question," meaning a question which is so worded as to suggest the desired answer. Jesus used this sort of query after the Pharisees had accused him of casting out demons by the power of Beelzebul. He asked, "If I cast out demons by Beelzebul, by whom do your sons cast them out?" (Matt. 12:27.) But Jesus made so little use of the leading question that we need give it no more consideration here. Socrates, not only made use of this sort of question, but, in a way, he even answered his own questions. This is something Jesus never did. His questions were stimulating; never were his hearers left mentally inert.

The questions asked by Jesus may be characterized as (1) direct questions, (2) indirect questions, and (3) hypothetical questions.

Let us first notice the direct question. The simple direct question is usually one that can be answered by "yes" or "no." Though the poorest of all questions for a teacher to use, it has a value in eliciting information. For this purpose Jesus asked of a demoniac, "What is your name?"

It has value in securing expressions of faith, as on some occasions when the sick sought healing, he asked a question like this, "Do you believe that I am able to do this?"

The Teacher found it helpful in commiting the pupil's mind definitely. So Jesus asked a very ill man, "Do you want to be healed?" The man's desire for healing was evident, but he explained the hindrances to the result he longed for.

The direct question assumes knowledge, and is useful in testing the degree of that knowledge. By thus learning the extent of the pupil's preparation, the teacher knows the point from which to proceed in giving further instruction.

Jesus used a type of direct question peculiar to himself. He used it to clarify confusion and uncertainty of knowledge in the minds of his hearers. A direct question would sometimes go to the heart of a problem and help the pupil to

46

see the truth more quickly than would a correct statement. To the Pharisees who, in trying Jesus, asked, "Is it lawful for a man to divorce his wife?" Jesus put the direct question, "What did Moses command you?" (Mark 10:2-3.) It opened up the way for clarifying the entire situation to the shame of the Pharisees. These were direct questions in the memorable conversation at Caesarea Philippi to which we have already referred. "Who do men say that the Son of man is?" (Matt. 16:13) and "Who do you say that I am?" (Matt. 16:15.) The first question prepared the way for the second, and the answer to the second was the clear statement, "You are the Christ, the Son of the living God." (Matt. 16:16.)

The indirect question requires for its answer, not only some knowledge but also activity of the mind. The facts of memory must be recalled and compared, and judgments formed. Jesus did not settle humanity's problems by answering all the questions of men. The Master raised problems before the minds of people, stirring minds and hearts to greater attainments in knowledge and character. Would men know him to be the Son of God? Yes, but they must learn it by indirect teaching.

To the Pharisees he put the indirect question, "What do you think of the Christ? Whose son is he?" When they answered, "The son of David," he put another question, then used a quotation from a Psalm, and asked another question.[1]

All through his ministry he taught in this way. On the day of his resurrection, when Mary stood by the open tomb weeping, he might have announced to her the news of his resurrection. But, no! He preferred to ask, "Why are you weeping? Whom do you seek?" (John 20:15.)

[1]See Matt. 22:41-46.

47

The hypothetical question puts before the mind a purely imaginary condition and calls for a statement of opinion based on this expressed condition. It is a very valuable means of teaching and was a favorite of the great Teacher's. The mind makes its decisions unhindered by personal considerations.

During his last week, the Master told two parables that are splendid illustrations for use here. In the first, the parable of the two sons, he states a hypothetic condition: Two sons were told to go work in a vineyard. One said, "I will not: but afterward he repented and went." The other said, " 'I go, sir,' but he did not go." Then Jesus asked the question, "Which of the two did the will of his father?" Jesus got their judgment that had been formed without prejudice: "The first." Then he gave them a needed rebuke, "Truly I say to you, the tax collectors and the harlots go into the kingdom of God before you." (Matt. 21:28-31.) He said more than these words, and told another parable—that of the wicked husbandmen.[2]

Sometimes he secured attention or aroused greater interest by an inquiry. Before telling the parable of the two sons, he asked, "What do you think?" He once asked, "With what can we compare the kingdom of God, or what parable shall we use for it?" Then he told the parable of the mustard seed.[3] Such questions were at times used as instructions to his most effective stories. When the pupil had the requisite information and the immediate action was desirable, the Teacher stimulated the feelings by a timely question. This was the effect of the thrice repeated query to Peter, "Simon, son of John, do you love me?"[4]

---

[2]Matt. 21:33-43.
[3]Mark 4:30-32.
[4]John 21:15-17.

The Master's questions were based on concrete illustrations; often they were put at the end of a story. When he had answered the lawyer's inquiry: "Who is my neighbor?" by a wonderful story of neighborliness,[5] Jesus asked, "Which of these three, do you think, proved neighbor to the man who fell among the robbers?" He made his pupils think and even express their thoughts; so by definite expression the impression made was deepened. And when a wrong answer was given, the Teacher could correct the mistake of the pupil.

The love that the Father has for his children and the provision made for them were taught by means of such questions as, "If God so clothes the grass of the field, which today is alive and tomorrow is thrown into the oven, will he not much more clothe you, O men of little faith?" (Matt. 6:30.) "What man of you, if his son asks him for a loaf, will give him a stone? Or if he asks for a fish, will give him a serpent?" (Matt. 7:9-10.) He taught Christian graces by the question method.

He taught love for enemies when he asked, "If you love those who love you, what reward have you? Do not even the tax collectors do the same?" (Matt. 5:46.) "And if you salute only your brethren, what more are you doing than others? Do not even the Gentiles do the same?" (Matt. 5:47.)

He taught obedience to God's will by his own example coupled with the question, "Shall I not drink the cup which the Father has given me?" (John 18:11.)

He taught the importance of faith when he exclaimed, "O men of little faith, why do you discuss among yourselves the fact that you have no bread?" (Matt. 16:8.) By means of

_____
[5]Luke 10:29-37.

49

questions he often rebuked his critics. By their use he often put them in a dilemma.

In his scathing rebukes to hypocrites, Jesus put some questions calculated to affect their seared consciences: "Which is greater, the gold or the temple that has made the gold sacred?" (Matt. 23:17.) "Which is greater, the gift or the altar that makes the gift sacred?" (Matt. 23:19.) In these two passages and in many others he rebuked the faultfinding of his enemies.

To them on another occasion he put the question, which accomplished both the purpose of a rebuke and the recalling of an Old Testament fact: "Have you never read what David did, when he was in need and was hungry, he and those who were with him: how he entered the house of God, when Abiathar was high priest, and ate the bread of the Presence, which it is not lawful for any but the priests to eat, and also gave it to those who were with him?" (Mark 2:25-26.)

So much was he given to this form of teaching that often in times of great emotion his feelings were expressed as questions: To some Pharisees he cried, "You brood of vipers! how can you speak good, when you are evil? For out of the abundance of the heart the mouth speaks." (Matt. 12:34.) And he expressed his surprise at the ignorance of a Jewish ruler when he said, "Are you a teacher of Israel, and yet you do not understand this?" (John 3:10.)

Questions were often put to Jesus. When the disciples came asking to know his reason for using parables, he gave a direct answer. When they had been disputing among themselves as to who was greatest in the kingdom, and came to him with the question, "Who is greatest in the kingdom of heaven?" he patiently gave answer. He first used an object lesson: a little child. Setting this child in the midst of the company, he said, "Unless you turn and become like children, you will never enter the kingdom of heaven." Then he gave a direct answer, "Whoever humbles himself like this child, he is the greatest in the kingdom of heaven." (Matt. 18:1-14.)

Sometimes the Master went beyond the question asked and taught other needed truths. In this instance he talked about children and stumbling blocks and God's will that none of these little ones perish. So profound was his knowledge of human nature that he was able to raise an isolated question to a high level from which he could teach some great principle of life and conduct.

Peter once asked, "Lord, how often shall my brother sin against me, and I forgive him? As many as seven times?" Jesus first gave a direct answer. "I do not say to you seven times, but seventy times seven." And at once the Teacher illustrated his words by telling the parable of the unmerciful servant. Then he made the application: "So also my heavenly Father will do to every one of you, if you do not forgive your brother from your heart." (Matt. 18:21-35.)

The Master knew the hearts of men better than they knew themselves, and he gladly helped those whose motives were right. In fact he even encouraged their questions. "Jesus knew that they wanted to ask him; so he said to them, 'Is this what you are asking yourselves, what I meant by saying, "A little while, and you will not see me, and again a little while, and you will see me"?' " (John 16:19.)

Sometimes, looking beyond the question at the questioner himself, he gave an answer that met the need of the inquirer's soul. His answer gave more than was asked. A lawyer asked, "Who is my neighbor?" The man was thinking in terms of a person—a neighbor—and Jesus answered by a parable that taught true neighborliness as well. He

51

was once asked, "Lord, will those who are saved be few?" He gave an answer that was an incentive to right living: "Strive to enter by the narrow door; for many, I tell you, will seek to enter and will not be able." (Luke 13:23-24.)

Many questions were put to the Teacher by his enemies. He treated all opponents frankly, gave them the sort of answers that their questions and spirit deserved, and utilized the opportunity thus afforded to teach valuable lessons to the multitudes.

The critics had noticed that the disciples of Jesus ignored the tradition of the elders in regard to ceremonial washing of hands before meals, and they came to Jesus asking the reason for this. He answered by rebuking them for exalting tradition above the commandment of God. Then he turned to the multitude and taught the meaning of real, as contrasted with this, ceremonial defilement.

Many a time his enemies were critical of his healing on the Sabbath and asked him such questions as this: "Is it lawful to heal on the sabbath?" He answered with a question and statement that shamed them, and he performed a miracle of healing.[6]

Again, "One sabbath he was going through the grainfields; and as they made their way his disciples began to pluck the ears of grain." The Pharisees said to him, "Look, why are they doing what is not lawful on the sabbath?" He answered by a reference in question form to the Scripture, and added, "The sabbath was made for man, and not man for the sabbath; so the Son of man is lord even of the sabbath." (Mark 2:23-28.)

Knowing men's hearts, there were times when he answered their unspoken questions. This was the case when he said to a paralytic, "My son, your sins are forgiven." When the

[6]Matt. 12:9-13.

52

scribes began to reason in their hearts, Jesus answered their thoughts and then healed the man.[7]

He was a guest in a Pharisee's home. During the meal the host began to reason within himself that his guest was surely no prophet, and Jesus answered the thought with plain, direct speech and a parable, and in the presence of the host, he forgave the sinful woman whose acts of faith had given rise to the Pharisee's wrong thoughts.[8]

From time to time, Jesus would answer his persecutors with questions they could not answer. Finally he silenced them until "no one was able to answer him a word, nor from that day did any one dare to ask him any more questions." (Matt. 22:46.)

[7]Mark 2:1-12.
[8]Luke 7:36-50.

8.

His Method of Using
the Scriptures

Every teacher of the Bible needs to know how the great Teacher used the Scriptures of his time. As a preface it is well to state that he was thoroughly versed in the sacred writings. It could not be otherwise when from childhood he was trained by Joseph and Mary and "increased in wisdom and stature, and in favor with God and man." (Luke 2:52.) Mary was a worthy mother. This would mean that she performed her duty and told her boy the stories of patriarchs, prophets, wise men, kings, and judges of the long ago. Joseph was a good man and so he would teach the boy the law of Moses, as did every Jewish father. When the child was five or six, his schooling in the synagogue began.

Until the age of ten, the child's textbook was the Bible. This was supplemented by the *Mishnah* or traditional law when he was ten. When he reached the age of fifteen, he could share in the discussions in the synagogue classrooms.

Here are two significant sentences worthy of the attention of modern parents, educators, and other teachers of religion: "Jewish education was conducted on what is now called the intensive plan. The home, the school, and the synagogue reinforced one another."[1] The Jews laid strong emphasis on the importance of education. It was in this sort of environment that Jesus grew to manhood.

His use of the Scriptures during his ministry shows a profound knowledge of all their sacred writings. He showed it when he taught and he showed it when dealing with the rabbis. The Old Testament of his day was divided into the law, the prophets, and the holy writings. He freely quoted from these and referred to them in a way that showed a deep, extensive knowledge. His training would also make him well acquainted with the traditions of the elders.

We begin this chapter, then, with the assurance that the Teacher had mastered his textbook. He was intimately acquainted with the glorious history of his race, with the heroic deeds of David and Joshua, the genius of Moses, the faith of Abraham, the wisdom of Solomon, and the devotion of David and Jonathan. He knew the beautiful clean life of Joseph, and the lovely story of Ruth and Naomi. He was familiar with law and poetry and prophecy, and he knew the hope of Israel for a coming Messiah. He knew this textbook.

His attitude toward it was always one of reverence and respect. He declared, "Think not that I have come to abolish the law and the prophets; I have come not to abolish them but to fulfil them. For truly, I say to you, till heaven and earth pass away, not an iota, not a dot, will pass from the law until all is accomplished. Whoever then relaxes one of the least of these commandments and teaches men so, shall be called least in the kingdom of heaven; but he who does them and teaches them shall be called great in the kingdom

---

[1]From *Jesus as a Teacher*, by B. A. Hinsdale (St. Louis: The Christian Publishing Co., 1895), p. 32.

of heaven." (Matt. 5:17-19.) He was a Jew, living under the law, and he respected it. When he healed a leper, he enjoined obedience to the law. He said, "Go, show yourself to the priest, and offer the gift that Moses commanded, for a proof to the people." (Matt. 8:4.)

These books he knew were books of religion, not of history or science. They recorded the heart of a great people, their sins, their virtues, their aspirations, their hopes. He ignored tradition, but he obeyed the commands.[2]

He quoted almost continuously from these Scriptures. He even answered the tempter in the wilderness by quoting several passages. The form of his quotations is of considerable interest. Most of the Old Testament was originally written in Hebrew, but a few centuries before the birth of Jesus, Hebrew became a dead language. It gave place to Aramaic. The result was that no Jew, unless he were a scholar, could read his Bible in the original. The situation was helped by the translation of the Septuagint out of the original Hebrew into Greek. It was made in Alexandria under Hebrew-Greek influences. The date was probably between 280 and 130 B.C. Sometimes Jesus seems to be quoting from the Septuagint and sometimes he gives very free renderings. His interest was not in the letter but in the spirit of the Books. He realized, what Paul later stated, that "the written code kills, but the Spirit gives life." (2 Cor. 3:6.) It was the reality, the content of Scripture, that he recognized as inspired. The Master often made allusions to the Law, the Hagiographa, and to the prophets Isaiah, Jeremiah, Daniel, Hosea, Joel, Micah, Zechariah, and Malachi.

[2]Matt. 17:24-27.

Not only did he quote from the Scriptures recognized by the Jews, and from the Law which was the only set of Books acknowledged by the Sadducees of his day and by the Samaritans, but he also referred to commentaries on these. He was well acquainted with the influential traditions of the Elders. There were other religious writings not in our Old Testament. These were called the Apocrypha. Because of expressions he used, it is evident that Jesus was acquainted with these books. They are a part of the Roman Catholic Bible but are not in the Bible of the Jews or Protestants.

Jesus, then, knew his textbook and he used it. He demonstrated the importance of both of these facts. One may know a book but not master it. So thoroughly did Jesus know the Scriptures that he needed no help of concordance or index but could quote at will. So filled was he with its content and spirit that it permeated his thoughts and found expression naturally in his words. His style of speech was that of his people and of the prophets of old, but his was finer.

His wisdom and proverbs were akin to those of Solomon, but far superior. Jesus once said, "The Queen of the South will arise at the judgment with this generation and condemn it; for she came from the ends of the earth to hear the wisdom of Solomon, and behold, something greater than Solomon is here." (Matt. 12:42). The wisdom of Solomon was worldly; that of Jesus was deeply spiritual.

Many of his ideas were in the Old Testament first. The Jewish conception of Jehovah, which prevails in these Scriptures, Jesus enlarged and beautified in his teaching of the fatherhood of God. Seventeen times in the Sermon on the Mount the term is used. Jehovah was for one people; the

57

Father loves all nations. Brotherhood was for one race, the Hebrews. Jesus goes much further and teaches that "whoever does the will of my Father in heaven is my brother, and sister, and mother." (Matt. 12:50.)

We have quoted his words in regard to fulfilment. Now we must understand them more clearly. The Sermon on the Mount furnishes the lesson, for seven times in this brief sermon he illustrates his idea. Each time he alludes to the Old Testament in the words, "You have heard that it was said," and then to the spiritual application with the words, "But I say to you." (Matt. 5:21-44.) First, he is dealing with murder and he shows that the fault lies in the moral condition back of it. Then he talks of adultery and declares that one who looks with impure intention is an adulterer at heart. In regard to one's word, the Teacher taught to keep it without swearing. He next speaks of the old law of vengeance, "An eye for an eye, and a tooth for a tooth," and leads up to the principle of long-suffering patience. Then the old teaching of love for neighbor and hatred for enemy, he broadened to love and prayer for enemies, too. In later teachings, he enjoined universal love and illustrated it by his life and death.

This idea of fulfilment would seem to be his thought when he said, "You search the scriptures, because you think that in them you have eternal life; and it is they that bear witness to me; yet you refuse to come to me that you may have life." (John 5:39-40.) When he visited Nazareth, his old home, he stood up in the synagogue one Sabbath day to read. He read Isaiah 61:1, 2. He made this application: "Today this scripture has been fulfilled in your hearing." (Luke 4:21.) With his dying breath on the cross, he cried, "It is finished." An apostle later on spoke of his "having canceled the bond which stood against us with its legal demands; this he set aside, nailing it to the cross." (Col. 2:14.) A well-known hymn writer, Philip P. Bliss, voices this sentiment in the words:

> Free from the law, O, happy condition,
> Jesus hath bled, and there is remission,
> Curs'd by the law and bruis'd by the fall,
> Grace hath redeemed us once for all.

> Now we are free—there's no condemnation,
> Jesus provides a perfect salvation;
> "Come unto Me," O, hear His sweet call,
> Come, and He saves us once for all.

Jesus was a student of prophecy. Who doubts that he visioned the glorious time foretold by Daniel?[3] Jesus talked continually about the kingdom. The Pharisees demanded that he tell when the kingdom would come. He answered them, "The kingdom of God is not coming with signs to be observed; nor will they say, 'Lo, here it is!' or 'There!' for behold, the kingdom of God is in the midst of you." (Luke 17:20-21.) Again, we see the principle of fulfilment.

His quotations from Scripture are made for the purpose of teaching. Though Jesus was not controversial, often the attitude of his opponents caused him to use the Scriptures as proof texts.

The rabbis, who were supposed to teach the law correctly, were not true to Moses in their teaching. They exalted tradition, and by their tradition they made void the word of God.

His teaching was unlike that of the scribes who quibbled over external matters, such as tithing mint, anise, and cummin, but left untouched the weightier matters of the law: justice, mercy, faith. They were particular about the ceremonial washing of hands and of jugs, cups, and pans, but

---

[3]Daniel 2:44, 45.

were slow to cleanse the heart and life. They were legalistic. Ritualism was greater with them than the truth. When they criticized the disciples for disregarding the tradition about the Sabbath, Jesus referred to the Book of 1 Samuel in question form: "Have you not read in the law?" (Matt. 12:5.) Then again to the same Pharisees he referred to a statement made by the prophet Hosea, saying, "If you had known what this means, 'I desire mercy, and not sacrifice,' you would not have condemned the guiltless." (Matt. 12:7.) When the Pharisees approached him with a question about divorce, he answered, "Have you not read?" and he referred to the beginning when God made them male and female.[4] To the Sadducees who questioned him about the resurrection, he said, "Have you not read?" and he quoted Exodus 3:6.[5] The Master followed the parable of the husbandmen with this same question, "Have you not read?" and quoted Psalm 118:22-23.

Many times Jesus referred to prophecies to prove that he was the Messiah. Even on the day of his resurrection, he continued this policy as he walked along with two disciples. He said, "O foolish men, and slow of heart to believe all that the prophets have spoken! Was it not necessary that the Christ should suffer these things and enter into his glory?" And beginning with Moses and all the prophets, he interpreted to them in all the scriptures the things concerning himself." (Luke 24:25-27.)

His quotations or references are usually given to make some truth clearer or to reinforce some statement he has made. After telling his disciples that he told parables to the people "because seeing they see not, and hearing they do not hear,

---

[4]Matt. 19:3-6. See Gen. 1:27; 5:2.
[5]Matt. 22:31.

60

nor do they understand" (Matt. 13:13), he stated that this was a fulfilment of prophecy. He referred to Isaiah 6:9-10.

Jesus interpreted anew the Scriptures of his people. They had been treated as a system of laws. He spiritualized them and stressed their essence as a revelation of God's plan.

The keynote of his greatest sermon seems to be the worth of spiritual as contrasted with vain things of sight. The truths that had been hidden behind ritualism and that were lost in their limited expressions, he expressed in a clear, positive, authoritative, and universal way.

What was his attitude toward the sacrificial system of the Old Testament? He attended the various feasts of the Jews where sacrifices were the rule.[6] This custom he used as a means of teaching a great spiritual truth, namely: right relations with your brother and love for him and for God.[7] This was better than burnt offerings. He said, "Go and learn what this means, 'I desire mercy, and not sacrifice.'" (Matt. 9:13.)

Strict adherence to the letter had caused the Pharisee to boast, "I fast twice a week, I give tithes of all that I get." (Luke 18:12.) But such people as he so far missed the real spirit of fasting that they disfigured their faces to call attention to their misery. Jesus called this "hypocrisy." The Scriptures of the Master's day only prescribed one fast day, the Day of Atonement. It is possible that the reference in Esther 4:3, 16 is to a fast instituted at a later time of great distress. The Jews had added many other such days, however, and frequent fasting had become a sign of devoutness. Jesus did not forbid it, but we note that his disciples refrained from it with his approval.[8]

---

[6]See John 4:45; 5:1; 6:4; 7:2; 11:55; 13:29; Luke 22:7.
[7]Matt. 5:23; Mark 12:33.
[8]Matt. 9:14-17.

When he talked of almsgiving, he made the truth clear that the giving should be in the right spirit, not for praise as was the custom of hypocrites.[9]

And when they prayed, their prayers were not to be for show as were those of hypocrites who prayed on street corners and in the synagogues for the purpose of having men see them. And in praying they should not follow the example of people who were guilty of useless repetitions thinking there was merit in much speaking.[10]

And so with fasting. If they were to fast, let it not be for show.[11]

[9]Matt. 6:1-4.
[10]Matt. 6:7.
[11]Matt. 6:16-18.

9.

His Use of the Case System

The method of the Master was largely the "case system." He called men singly, or in small groups, to follow him. He spent a night in prayer before selecting just twelve men to become apostles. He sent out these twelve, and later seventy others, on a special mission, grouping them in pairs—one personality to supplement another.

In his miracles of healing, he never healed a multitude at once. A nobleman's son and Peter's mother-in-law, he healed of fever. He cured a leper, and at another time ten lepers. A palsied man in a home and another, a centurion's servant, an impotent man, and a man with a withered hand were healed. A woman was cured of an affliction of twelve years' duration. Several blind men were given their sight. He raised from the dead a widow's only son, a ruler's only daughter, and his friend Lazarus. Seven times he cast demons out of individuals.

Even in his miracles of feeding the multitudes, he was prompted by compassion for the individuals. He said, "I have compassion on the crowd, because they have been with me now three days, and have nothing to eat; and I am unwilling to send them away hungry, lest they faint on the way." (Matt. 15:32.)

The personal attentions he gave the poor and the sick and the bereaved are a reproach to men who can think only in terms of the masses. The complications of modern life have resulted in the tendency to grant relief impersonally.

This personal relation is essential. When he would teach love for people, Jesus did not teach affection in the abstract. He taught the love of one person for another person. Heart answers to heart. Genuine love for the distant heathen is tested by the quality of one's love for the heathen at one's door. The test of Christian love is in its personal application.

Personality was precious to Jesus. His healing and his teaching and his miracles of deliverance when he stilled the wind and the sea, or when he took the hand of Peter and kept him from sinking in the sea, were expressions of this love. He even prayed for men by name. He said to Peter, "I have prayed for you that your faith may not fail." (Luke 22:32.)

This interest in individuals did not keep Jesus away from large centers of population, for much of his ministry was in such places. Even when away from the cities he was likely to be followed by thousands. He taught the multitudes. All of this is true, and yet Jesus did not think of them en masse. It seems safe to state that his interest in the crowds is the interest of one who sees the individuals in it. He knew crowd psychology, by whatever name it may be called, and was not deceived. The Master was thinking primarily of individuals. He so taught as to develop personality—the personality of the individual man or woman.

He taught the love of God for the individual. In the parable of the lost sheep, it was the one lost sheep that the shepherd sought in the wilderness. It was over finding the one that the shepherd was filled with rejoicing. In his application, Jesus said, "Even so, I tell you, there will be more joy in heaven over one sinner who repents than over ninety-nine righteous persons who need no repentance." (Luke 15:7.) It was the one piece of silver that the woman in the parable sought for diligently and continued her search until she found. Jesus likened her joy to that in heaven. "Even so, I tell you, there is joy before the angels of God over one sinner who repents." (Luke 15:10.) The father of the prodigal was overjoyed when the one that was lost came home.[1]

What the Master gave to individuals, he desired them to share with other individuals. To the apostles he said, "As the Father has sent me, even so I send you." (John 20:21.) He left no writings, no elaborate organizations, but he left a group of individuals trained by him for the task. To them he gave the Great Commission—a commission to all nations, it is true, but comprehending the individual. The Gospel could not be understood and obeyed except as individual minds and hearts responded.

In his teaching the Master used the principle of adaptation, now recognized as one of the fundamental principles underlying all teaching. This simply means that the teaching, in matter and method, must be continually adapted to the pupil. With his changing interests and powers must come different matter and method. Jesus did this as he taught his growing disciples. We shall see his use of this principle when we note his manner of meeting the needs of certain individuals.

Teaching must be adapted to the pupil's capacity. To do this necessitates a thorough acquaintance with the pupil. Jesus knew people. He knew mind and he knew minds.

[1]Luke 15:11-32.

Many times his biographers speak of his knowledge and insight: "He knew all men and needed no one to bear witness of man; for he himself knew what was in man." (John 2:24-25.) "Jesus, knowing their thoughts, said, 'Why do you think evil in your hearts?'" (Matt. 9:4.) "Knowing their thoughts, he said unto them, 'Every kingdom divided against itself is laid waste." (Matt. 12:25.) "When Jesus perceived their questionings, he answered them, 'Why do you question in your hearts?'" (Luke 5:22.) "He knew their thoughts." (Luke 6:8.) "Jesus perceived the thought of their hearts." (Luke 9:47.)

When men came with the wrong motive, he knew their hypocrisy. Once he asked, "Why put me to the test?" (Mark 12:15.) He could tell those who had faith in him, "For Jesus knew from the first who those were that did not believe, and who it was that should betray him." (John 6:64.) Having such knowledge and intuition, from a pedagogical viewpoint this was a prime source of his power. He was able to meet the demands of every occasion. He was never surprised, never confused. He always grasped the right conditions for teaching.

Included in the Master's knowledge of people must be his thorough acquaintance with their daily lives. His disciples he knew intimately from friendly companionship, with all that this involves. He knew other people from mingling with them in homes, at feasts, in social gatherings, on the streets, in the synagogue, in the temple. He knew their religious attitudes. He knew the political situation and the hopes of Israel. His interest was more in life than in theory.

Again, when we say Jesus knew men, we include more knowledge than that of the intellect. Lesser teachers have often thought they knew people when they understood their mental attitudes. Such teachers consider that an appeal to the thinking processes is sufficient. Proof is all they attempt. A logical argument is their entire procedure. They forget that spiritual things are spiritually discerned. Others exclude the feelings partially at least in their teaching. There are great religious truths too deep for reasoning. The affections play a large part in life. A lecturer once said, "It is a mistake to say we act from reason. We really act emotionally, and then seek reason to defend our actions." This is quite often our procedure.

The friendly companionship of Jesus enabled him to get very close to people. This was especially true of the twelve who were his constant companions in his varied experiences, but it was also the case with others. He called his disciples friends and children. Sometimes he would take them away from the crowds. "He said to them, 'Come away by yourselves to a lonely place, and rest a while.' For many were coming and going, and they had no leisure even to eat. And they went away in the boat to a lonely place by themselves." (Mark 6:31, 32. See also Mark 3:7.) The Master had special talks with these chosen ones.

He called a woman "daughter"; and once a blind man and again a woman—Mary Magdalene—spoke to him by the name "Rabboni," my teacher. He was so friendly as to invite himself to the home of Zacchaeus. He often visited the Bethany home of Martha, Mary, and Lazarus. He was sufficiently approachable to be called by his enemies "a friend of tax collectors and sinners." It was easy for him, then, to find the point of contact so essential to instruction, and then to fit the lesson to the pupil's capacity and need.

Before we consider a few specific cases, it is well that we know the general method adopted by the Master in dealing with individuals. We have learned that he found the point of contact and gave instruction according to the capacity and need of each pupil.

He considered their mental disposition. Were they hostile, indifferent, or eager for truth? Were they so spiritually limited in capacity that his meaning could not be easily comprehended? What were their moral dispositions? Was their limitation emotional?

He used the Scriptures, the world of nature, the behavior of men—in fact a wide range of objects and facts—to help the learners. He told parables according to their capacity to hear. Mark says, "With many such parables he spoke to them, as they were able to hear it." (Mark 4:33.)

He used these two great teaching principles: First, the material and method must be adapted to the pupil; second, the material and method must be such as to help attain the desired end.

He taught not to impart facts that might lie dormant in the mind, but to transform lives. This expression of his represented his aim: "Every one then who hears these words of mine and does them." (Matt. 7:24.) His teaching "took effect" in the lives of all who sat at his feet. In his teaching Jesus showed eagerness to help the pupil grasp a rule or principle. He was less anxious to settle the particular matter before them.

It is well that we devote some time to the analysis of a few cases. Let us listen as he teaches a woman of Samaria. The setting is interesting. It is noontime. Jesus, a Jew, is sitting by a well in Samaria. Prejudice generally led the Jewish travelers to avoid Samaria, but Jesus is without prejudice. As he sits there, a Samaritan woman approaches to draw water.

At once Jesus grasps an opportunity to teach. The point of contact must first be established, and this he does by asking a favor, "Give me a drink." By this beginning, the Master has done several things. First, he has used the element of surprise. He, a Jew, actually speaks to a woman. The rabbis taught that it was beneath them to talk with an "inferior creature." There was a morning prayer in which a Jew would thank God "who hath not made me a Gentile, a slave, or a woman." The woman's surprise was great because this Jew spoke not only to a woman, but to a Samaritan woman, "For Jews have no dealings with Samaritans." (John 4:9.)

Further, Jesus helped establish the point of contact by referring to water. She knew the need of water. Her interest was there, for had she not come to draw water? Thus he used a concrete object to begin the conversation.

His means of approach was friendly. He asked a favor. He would put himself under obligation to her. The woman showed her surprise. She asked, "How is it that you a Jew, ask a drink of me, a woman of Samaria?" He answered by a reference to living water with the suggestion that he could supply it. This quickened her interest as it also aroused her curiosity. He was leading from the concrete to the abstract but she did not know what he meant at all. She was still thinking of the water in the well below them. Jesus patiently explained it as "a spring of water welling up to eternal life."

The Teacher then made the application personal. "Go," said he, "call your husband, and come here." The conversation immediately revealed the fact that Jesus knew the woman's past and present, though he accused her of no sin. We see how the Master is using the conversational method to draw out truths and expressions of opinion and to lead on to his object. The woman begins to learn. Now she knows

One greater than an ordinary Jew is talking with her, for she says, "Sir, I perceive that you are a prophet."

To this prophet, who has won her interest, respect, and friendship and who has aroused her curiosity, she raises the question of the place of worship. The Jews worshiped in Jerusalem, the Samaritans at Mount Gerizim. In his answer, the Teacher explains that God is spirit, that true worship is not confined to a city or a mountain. It is not a matter of location, but one of the spirit, for "those who worship him must worship in spirit and truth."

Now very rapidly, from an unpromising beginning, this woman's understanding of spiritual things has been so well developed that Jesus is able to teach another fact. She refers to the anticipated coming of the Messiah who "will show us all things." Then to this Samaritan woman Jesus makes the announcement, probably the first time he has ever made it: "I who speak to you am he." How well did Jesus teach! Good teaching leads to right action. The woman became a messenger of good news to her people. Soon, upon her testimony, many Samaritans came to him, and he talked with them. Many were won to the truth, at first because of the woman's word, and then because of the Teacher's own message.

Let us consider another case. A young man ran to the Master and said, "Teacher, what good deed must I do to have eternal life?" (Matt. 19:16.) In helping this inquirer, Jesus first explained that none is good save one, even God.

Then he taught by the use of the man's knowledge of the law. He said, "Keep the commandments." The conversational method was used throughout. When the man asked which commandments, Jesus said, "You shall not kill. You shall not commit adultery. You shall not steal. You shall not bear false witness. Honor your father and your mother, and, You shall love your neighbor as yourself." The young man said, "All these things I have observed."

But this man, faithful as he had been to these duties, was conscious of something wrong. "What do I still lack?" he asked. The love of the Master went out to him, so eager for the best was he and yet so possessed by one great fault. Jesus spoke these words: "If you would be perfect, go, sell what you possess and give to the poor, and you will have treasure in heaven; and come, follow me." The Teacher knew the idol that had kept the life from being perfect. "When the young man heard this he went away sorrowful; for he had great possessions." (Matt. 19:16-22.)

How different the method of Jesus from many a modern teacher! The danger is that one will tell the inquirer a list of things to do and leave the real self untouched. What matters attention to rules if the heart is far from the right? Jesus enabled this questioner to see his real self.

Not to every one would the Master have given the same instruction. His attitude toward wealth was never such as to make its possession always a sin. But this young man had the great fault that could be cured only by the drastic treatment prescribed.

Jesus used this incident as an occasion to teach his disciples a strong lesson on the peril of riches, coupled with the thought-provoking statement: "It will be hard for a rich man to enter the kingdom of heaven." (Matt. 19:23.)

Three interesting cases of bitter opposition are recorded by Matthew. The first is that of the Pharisees who counseled together as to how they might ensnare him in his talk. They selected the Herodians to make the attack.

As a background for this incident we must remind ourselves that the Jews were subject to Rome at this time and were, of course, using Roman money and paying taxes.

There was a strongly divided sentiment among the Jews as to their duty in this matter. The Herod party favored the paying of taxes. Now they come to Jesus with words of flattery, saying, "Teacher, we know that you are true, and teach the way of God truthfully, and care for no man; for you do not regard the position of men." (Matt. 22:16.) Then they put their carefully prepared catch question, "Tell us, then, what you think. Is it lawful to pay taxes to Caesar, or not?"

Jesus was not to be trapped. Perceiving their wickedness, he asked, "Why put me to the test, you hypocrites?" Then he proceeded to catch them. "Show me the money for the tax," he said. They brought him a coin. He made them supply the object to lead to their discomfiture. He said to them, "Whose likeness and inscription is this?" When they gave the inevitable answer, "Caesar's," he practically compelled their acknowledgment of obligation to the Roman government. It was money of the government that they were using. Then he gave his answer to the question with which they began, "Render therefore to Caesar the things that are Caesar's, and to God the things that are God's." What fault could any find with this reply? They marveled at his answer and went away.

But it was a time of bitter opposition, a time when opposing parties would work toward the same end. That same day the Sadducees tested him. This sect of the Jews did not believe in a resurrection, and now they base their catch question on this subject. Flattering words seemed to have been omitted from this conversation.

They began by referring to a command in the law, saying, "Teacher, Moses said, 'If a man dies, having no children, his brother must marry the widow, and raise up children for his brother.'" (Matt. 22:24.) Then these Sadducees told a

72

story of seven brothers. The first married, and died childless. The second married the widow. He died childless. So in turn each brother became the husband of this woman and died childless. Last of all, the woman died. Then the "hard" question was put: "In the resurrection, therefore, to which of the seven will she be wife? For they all had her."

In his answer, the Master proceeded to show up their ignorance of Scripture and of the power of God, "For in the resurrection they neither marry nor are given in marriage, but are like angels in heaven." This answer was made exceedingly interesting by the knowledge that the Sadducees did not believe in angels any more than they believed in the resurrection.

Then the Teacher further emphasized the continuance of life after death by the statement, "And as for the resurrection of the dead, have you not read what was said to you by God, 'I am the God of Abraham, and the God of Isaac, and the God of Jacob'? He is not God of the dead, but of the living." And as Jesus put to shame these persecutors, the multitudes were astonished at his teaching.[2]

When the Pharisees learned how effectively the Teacher had silenced the Sadducees, they had another conference, with the result that one of their number, a lawyer, tested him with this question, "Teacher, which is the great commandment in the law?" (Matt. 22:36.) Or as Mark puts it, "Which commandment is the first of all?" (Mark 12:28-34.)

Going beyond the Ten Commandments he answered, "You shall love the Lord your God with all your heart, and with all your soul, and with all your mind, and with all your strength." The lawyer had asked for no other commandment, but just as if he were reading the unneighborly spirit actuating this lawyer, Jesus adds: "The second is this, You

[2]Matt. 22:23-33.

73

shall love your neighbor as yourself." And Mark adds: "There is no other commandment greater than these."

The lawyer was made to see and to acknowledge that love is everything—more than burnt offerings and sacrifices. The Master had evidently helped the lawyer to a correct viewpoint and to a better spiritual condition, for Jesus said to him, "You are not far from the kingdom of God."

We close this chapter with an incident in the Bethany home to which Jesus so often resorted in the days of turmoil. He loved Lazarus and his two sisters, Martha and Mary. His welcome was always assured. On the day of which we are thinking, Martha had given him a welcome and was busy about serving. In fact she was "distracted with much serving." (Luke 10:40.) Mary, on the contrary, was happy in listening to the word of the Guest as she sat at his feet.

Martha was a choice spirit, but her irritable feelings finally got the better of her and she went to Jesus with the question, "Lord do you not care that my sister has left me to serve alone? Tell her then to help me." This would be a discourteous remark to a guest in any home, but especially in an Oriental home, and to such a Guest. But Jesus knew Martha. She was genuine. Her love expressed itself in active service. And he knew that she was distracted. Of course he cared, he whose heart was filled with compassion for the multitudes who seemed as sheep without a shepherd; he who calmed the fears of his frightened disciples when he stilled the stormy winds and waves on the Sea of Galilee; he whose compassion led him to heal the sick, raise the dead, and preach the good news to all classes. Yes, he cared, and Martha really knew it.

This good woman has sometimes been censured as being too materialistic, yet when death entered this home, it was Martha who first knew of her Lord's approach and ran to

74

meet him with a cry of trust and welcome, while "Mary sat in the house." (John 11:20.) Both women looked to him as their Teacher, and more. It was Martha who voiced faith in his deity: "I believe that you are the Christ, the Son of God, he who is coming into the world." (John 11:27.)

It is not surprising, then, that the Guest, so definitely challenged, replied kindly, "Martha, Martha, you are anxious and troubled about many things: one thing is needful. Mary has chosen the good portion, which shall not be taken away from her." (Luke 10:41-42.)

He was sympathetic and he understood both of his friends. In his answer, he showed no offended dignity, but only the kind heart of a discerning friend. In his great Sermon on the Mount he had warned the multitudes about anxiety over things of lesser importance, and had urged that the kingdom of God and his righteousness be sought first. And Martha was always his loyal disciple.

10.

His Use of the Developing Method

Teaching has been defined as the process by which one mind produces the life-unfolding processes in another. The teacher's task is to arouse and direct the self-activities of the pupils. He is to tell nothing the pupil can learn for himself. The aim is self-guidance. The pupil must be helped toward the control of his own thoughts, feelings, and actions. Self-activity, the activity that originates with self, enlists the whole being. It is the greatest law ever discovered in teaching. It is basic. Teaching that does not arouse self-activity is a failure.

Jesus used the developing method with the utmost skill throughout his entire ministry. In the first place, he possessed all the requisite qualities.

He knew people, their thoughts, their lives. In spite of this knowledge he was optimistic and prophesied great things for humanity and the kingdom of God.

He possessed the love and faith and patience necessary as well as the wisdom to deal with each person as the need required.

He loved the truth he would teach, and so by his life he did most effective teaching.

Academic teaching aims to impart knowledge. The object of Christian teaching is Christian character. Jesus knew the importance of personal friendships between himself and those he would influence for good. Some were bound to him by gratitude for healing, some for food, some for kind words, and some for his friendliness and his beautiful way of showing them spiritual truths. He set a perfect example for modern leaders who would give his message and develop lives. He loved the people. They loved him. Their wills were moved by his strong will. Many a character developed Godward because he had been with Jesus.

The Master's aim was not to fill his pupil's minds with facts, but so to stimulate as to awaken and direct their mental processes. He also aimed to help mold their emotional lives and stimulate to right desires and right behavior.

A few years ago psychologists divided psychic activity into three classes: knowing, feeling, and willing. Now they recognize the fact that each self is possessed of mind and emotions and will but that these faculties and activities are not as independent of each other as was thought formerly. However, if we bear in mind this explanation, we will find it profitable to consider separately the effect of the Teacher's developing method on mind and emotions and voluntary behavior.

Without mentioning intellect or sensibility or will, Jesus treated people as capable of thinking, feeling, and voluntarily doing. He talked of sowing seed and he talked of harvest. In his teaching processes, he was willing to sow the good seed and give it time to germinate, to strike its roots deeply into the soil, and grow until the harvest. His teaching method called for responsive effort on man's part. Its effects were

77

not produced at once, but they were more and more lasting as the life developed in its Christian beauty and holiness.

Often Jesus refrained from giving certain instruction because of the mental or emotional, and, we may add, the spiritual limitations of the people. Once he said, "Not all men can receive this precept." (Matt. 19:11.) And again in regard to his parables, it is reported that he "spoke the word to them, as they were able to hear it." (Mark 4:33. See John 7:17.) After about three years of training the twelve, Jesus said, "I have yet many things to say to you, but you cannot bear them now." (John 16:12.) One must have an open mind, a will to learn, if he is to grasp the truth.

Jesus carefully adapted his material and methods to the state of development of the pupil. He always obeyed the pedagogic law: From the known to the unknown. The truth to be taught must always be learned through the truth already known. We may say he used a system of graded lessons, for he talked to each as his development warranted. He carefully selected material, repeated the lessons, and helped in the slow processes of growth.

His method was the method of nurture. He put his disciples where they could see and hear the truths he would have them grasp. He gave them many object lessons. He had many heart-to-heart talks with them as a group and with some individually. Peter, James, and John were given special opportunities on the Mount of Transfiguration, and on other occasions. And thus they grew. Gradually under his loving guidance they were becoming more able to grasp great spiritual truths.

Jesus would assign special tasks to the twelve, involving experience in work for the kingdom. He tested their work and their knowledge. His gift to them was not one of form but of life. He said, "The words that I have spoken to you are spirit and life." (John 6:63.) Again he said, "I came that they may have life, and have it abundantly." (John 10:10.) He sought to communicate the things of real life—vitality, character.

The Master had regard for the order of mental growth. In his use of the developing method he followed the method of nature. He called to the mind's attention only that for which it was prepared, and as its capacity increased, his subject matter was accordingly changed. With growth and knowledge came increased ability for growth and knowledge.

In moulding the thought life of his pupils, he adopted what Dr. Neander calls "accommodation." He never overestimated the power of the mind. He gave it only enough matter for its capacity and matter of the sort it could grasp. He did not believe that all truth should be taught on every occasion and to every person. He used the expressions common to their everyday life.

He raised no issue on history or science, though he must have been conscious of the errors in many of their ideas. He used the language of his day when he spoke of heaven as above and Hades as below, or when he said "the sun was risen," or stated that the queen of the south came from "the ends of the earth." He accommodated his expression to theirs when he spoke of the mustard seed as "less than all the seeds."

In moulding their thought life, Jesus imparted information. He did not always wait until the need for their knowledge arose, but he gave it in advance of the need. The Sermon on the Mount illustrates this truth. In it he dwelt on the sin and folly of worry. This had a bearing on the lives of his people, for they were likely to become anxious. He met the general needs of his hearers. Then, of course, there was information needed by certain individuals. He

79

was glad to teach each mind as the problem presented itself. Then, again, special methods were needed to make religious truth clear to the mind, and these he used freely, adopting the law of accommodation continually.

But the imparting of information was by no means his sole desire. He wished to stir up the mental activity of his pupils. For this reason, the Master sometimes withheld information, but asked questions and left the hearers to think out the answers. When their answers were wrong, he corrected them. Especially was this true of their ideas of the kingdom. Time after time he patiently taught the truth about the kingdom that is not "coming with signs to be observed." (Luke 17:20.)

He changed their method of thinking. He gave them new conceptions of God, of the Messiah, of the kingdom, and of man's relation to God and man.

Jesus recognized the fact that growth depends upon the contents and condition of the mind. This is a law of nature. The parable of the talents illustrates the working of this law. His paradoxical conclusion was: "For to every one who has will more be given, and he will have abundance; but from him who has not, even what he has will be taken away." (Matt. 25:29.) Action leads to power; inaction to loss of power. Jesus knew that action gave power to thought and so he endeavored to make his disciples understand the importance of doing things. He wished them to think for themselves; then act or not as their thoughts directed.

The Teacher used the developing method in dealing with the emotional life of his pupils. We must not forget that while knowing, feeling, and willing are all forms of mental activity, they are not all equally prominent at the same time. To make this clear we need simply remind the reader of the effect of violent emotion on one's thinking faculty.

It is by no means true that people will live right if they know the right. Education of the intellect does not mean a better man. The fact is emotion leads to action.

Jesus approached the emotions through the intellect. He knew that men would act because they felt, and they would act in accord with their feelings. And so he made it his aim to arouse in his hearers those feelings that would lead to right behavior.

Sometimes he influenced their own emotions by telling of his. He spoke of his compassion for the multitudes. At other times he showed his compassion by healing the sick. He expressed his love for little children. He spoke emotionally in his rebukes to the Pharisees. This was especially true in his eloquent speech recorded by Matthew. In these cases of scathing rebuke, his purpose was evidently to weaken the influence of the Jewish leaders who were opposing his mission for humanity. He enlisted the sympathy of his little group when he said, "My soul is very sorrowful, even to death." (Matt. 26:38.) Even the look he gave Peter on the night of the betrayal stirred that disciple so deeply that "he went out and wept bitterly." (Luke 22:62.)

Great was the emotion of the twelve when their leader was about to leave them. He said, "Let not your hearts be troubled." (John 14:1.) He then spoke comfortingly and at the same time appealed to their minds as he spoke of the Father's house. Again, he promised to send another teacher, the Holy Spirit, who would guide them into all truth. He was thus preparing them to act bravely and intelligently and according to the Christian principles he had been teaching throughout these years of their association together.

Jesus was not afraid of emotion based on fact. He, the possessor of the greatest thought power the world has known, possessed strong feelings also. He could love deeply and was not afraid to say so. Even when he prayed in their presence, he poured out his heart to the Father on their behalf. He told a stranger about God's love in what we call the golden text of the Bible: "For God so loved the world that he gave his only Son, that whoever believes in him should not perish but have eternal life." (John 3:16.)

He had strong feelings toward those who would put stumbling blocks in the way of children, and he said so in forceful words. When he talked with the seeker after truth or the penitent, he plainly showed his tenderness of feeling when he spoke. What more yearning love could one ask than that he showed for Jerusalem when he wept over the city that knew not the day of her visitation. His emotion on the cross was heartbreaking. He cried, "My God, my God, why hast thou forsaken me?" (Matt. 27:46.) When his limp body hung lifeless on the cross and men came to take him down, one drove a spear into his side and "there came out blood and water." (John 19:34.) "He came to his own home, and his own people received him not." (John 1:11.) And he died of a broken heart!

Jesus nurtured the emotional life of others. The twelve were with him during those emotional months when the lame and blind and diseased were crying out for help or shouting from excitement and joy when they healed. They were present during the emotional times when enemies sought to take him. Three of the number witnessed the transfiguration and were also present in Gethsemane on that night when he prayed in agony. Many of the parables depicted emotion. The Teacher used emotional experiences to teach right lessons, build character, and influence the will to act accordingly.

Let us not forget as we watch our Leader use the developing method, that he was developing the whole self and not simply the emotions. We must remember that this entire self acts in three ways: intellectually, emotionally, and as a will.

Socrates took it as a certainty that if a person knew the right he would do it. This Greek philosopher, we now know, was mistaken.

The Romans worked on the sensibilities of their hearers. One need only read their great orations to see how they appealed to the feelings.

But Jesus sought to influence the will. Through the intellect and the emotions, he endeavored so to develop souls as to move the will to act.

Spiritual truth lies deeper than intellectual proof. The understanding is important in matters of believing and living, but it is an error to exclude the heart, even partially. Real teaching will always touch these three. It causes the affections to be centered upon what is worth while. T. T. Brumbaugh refers to an address delivered on Puerto Rico. At its conclusion, a boy arose and said, "I now know better than before the needs of these people. I feel that we ought to help them. I move that we send ten dollars to Puerto Rico to help the work." Here we have it in brief: "I know, I feel, I move."

How did Jesus use the developing method with Simon Peter? In this case, as in all real teaching, it was a process by which one mind (in this instance, the mind of the Master) set to work with a definite purpose to produce the life-unfolding process in another.

Jesus had a difficult task before him, but he was aided by his sympathy and love for Peter. Peter knew this and he knew that the Master prayed for him by name.[1]

[1] Luke 22:32.

The records introduce him as Simon, Andrew's brother. He was of the motor type, impulsive and rash. He spoke up when others were silent. When Jesus asked the twelve, "Who do you say that I am?" (Matt. 16:15), it was Peter who answered. When Jesus talked about suffering and being killed, it was bold Peter who rebuked him.[2] When, with James and John, he accompanied his Lord to the Mount of Transfiguration, he alone of the three spoke out and said to Jesus, "Lord, it is well that we are here; if you wish, I will make three booths here, one for you and one for Moses and one for Elijah." (Matt. 17:4.) When Jesus proceeded to wash the feet of the disciples on that night of the betrayal, Peter was the one to object. And when his Master said, "If I do not wash you, you have no part in me" (John 13:8), then Peter went to the other extreme and said, "Lord, not my feet only but also my hands and my head!" (John 13:9.) His voice was the most insistent in declaring, "Even if I must die with you, I will not deny you." (Matt. 26:35.) That same night in his boldness, he rashly cut off a man's ear.

Despite this boldness, fear was an emotion quite prominent in Peter's character. Fear prompted him to run away when Jesus was made a prisoner; fear caused him to deny his Lord with cursing and swearing. When he began to sink into the Sea of Galilee, he was so afraid that he cried out, "Lord, save me." (Matt. 14:30.)

It would seem then that Peter was a man of strong emotions, but unstable. He possessed the quality of leadership without the steadiness of a good leader. He was not the first man selected as an apostle, yet Matthew gives him first prominence in naming the twelve.[3] When those receiving

[2]Matt. 16:21-22.
[3]Matt. 10:2.

the tribute money in Capernaum wanted to know the Master's custom in regard to this tax, they asked Peter about it.[4]

Jesus kept Peter near him and taught him as he was able to understand. When Simon questioned his Master about taking a servant's place and asked, "Lord, do you wash my feet?" Jesus knew Peter was not yet prepared to realize the full meaning of the lesson. So he answered, "What I am doing you do not know now, but afterward you will understand." That night the Master said to the group, and to this disciple as well, "I have yet many things to say to you, but you cannot bear them now." (John 16:12.) For some time he had been talking of his coming suffering, emphasizing its certainty and meaning.

Jesus helped Peter through kindly service in the home, curing his wife's mother of a fever. He rebuked Simon in strong words, and yet he was always helping this pupil to learn and grow stronger and get his emotions under better control. He was helping his pupil find himself.

Jesus corrected Peter for using the sword. He said, "All who take the sword will perish by the sword." (Matt. 26:52.)

Long before Simon was rocklike in character, the Teacher gave him a new name: Cephas, Peter,[5] which means rock. It was a fine suggestion, but it was long before he became a rock.

Again, Peter was narrow. He was trained to look upon a large portion of the people as common and unclean. It is true that in his sermon on the day of Pentecost, he said, "For the promise is to you and to your children and to all that are far off, every one whom the Lord our God calls to him." (Acts 2:39.) But he was slow to understand that

[4]Matt. 17:24.
[5]John 1:42.

85

Gentiles were included. It took a vision on the housetop, coupled with God's blessings to a devout Gentile, to broaden him.[6]

Jesus never forgot this pupil. Even on the day of his resurrection he appeared to Peter. That day the angel in the tomb sent a message to the disciples, and to Peter by name.[7]

Early one morning, after the resurrection, Jesus and seven of his disciples were partaking of breakfast together. Peter was there. After they had finished eating, the Lord began a conversation with this disciple, a conversation that has been called the most rigid examination ever given a candidate for the Christian ministry. The Teacher used the question method, three times asking Simon if he loved him. Three times the disciple answered in the affirmative. And each time received a command.[8] Thrice had Simon denied his Lord and now he thrice confessed him and three times he has been entrusted with a big task. If Simon loved Jesus, he would serve him and this love would be his inspiration to serve. Jesus did not rebuke him except in this gentle way. He loved Simon and wanted his love.

He believed in Peter and wanted him to be rocklike. After the testing the Master made a prophecy, " 'Truly, truly, I say to you, when you were young, you girded yourself and walked where you would; but when you are old, you will stretch out your hands, and another will gird you and carry you where you do not wish to go.' (This he said to show by what death he was to glorify God.) And after this he said to him, 'Follow me.' " (John 21:18-19.)

Ten days after the ascension, Peter and the rest of the apostles, baptized in the Holy Spirit, preached boldly and

[6]Acts 10:9-16. See Acts 10:1—11:18.
[7]Mark 16:7.
[8]John 21:15-17.

effectively, and thousands were converted. Not once was Peter vacillating or fearful. When persecutions came, he endured bravely and spoke boldly. He with the other apostles was beaten, but he remained firm. When James was beheaded and Peter was in prison expecting a like fate, no doubt, he slept the deep sleep of the trustful and was not awakened even by the brightness of an angel's presence. In fact he did not wake until the angel smote his side. Tradition reports his death on the cross. It is said that he asked to be crucified with his head down because he was unworthy to suffer as did his Lord.

Did Peter learn the lesson of nonresistance taught him that night he had drawn a sword? See him with the company of disciples after he and John had been released by the council. They lifted up their voices in prayer; not in prayer for vengeance but for boldness to speak the word and for miraculous power.[9]

It would profit us to study other lives Jesus developed. We would find, as with Peter, that the change would be great because "they had been with Jesus."

James and John were the sons of Zebedee. Jesus surnamed them "Boanerges," meaning, "sons of thunder." And they did not belie their names.

They sought the highest place in the earthly kingdom they expected him to establish. There was a time when the people in a village of Samaritans would not receive Jesus "because his face was set toward Jerusalem." (Luke 9:53.) When James and John learned this, their indignation and unforbearing spirits were expressed in the question, "Lord, do you want us to bid fire come down from heaven and consume them?" But Jesus rebuked them and taught them

[9]Acts 4:23-31.

87

better. Apparently untroubled, he led these men to another village.

All through his ministry he helped these disciples. They heard him say, "Love your enemies" (Matt. 5:44), and they saw his proofs of love.

Did they learn? Yes. John was called "the disciple that Jesus loved." His writings are full of the subject. They had heard Jesus say, "Greater love has no man than this, that a man lay down his life for his friends." (John 15:13.) James died a martyr's death, and John lived to an old age, testifying to the love of God and proving his steady devotion.

11.

His Use of Attention

Many eminent psychologists have stated that teaching is the art of securing attention, but this cannot be true. There can really be no teaching until attention has been secured, and teaching ceases when attention is lost. We may define teaching, then, as the art of using attention.

It is imperative therefore that the teacher know what influences hinder and what agencies help secure and hold the attention. Until the pupil is attentive, the teacher will make a mistake to proceed with the lesson. If the mental attitude of the pupil is wrong, instruction is impossible.

First, there are some hindrances to attention. The pupil who is in poor physical condition or who is in a room improperly ventilated is kept from hearing with understanding.

Disturbances, such as are made by persons moving about the room, rattling papers, or whispering, are hindrances.

Some pupils are not mentally prepared to attend to a subject. This may be due to the mind's limited capacity or to the presence of disturbing causes such as worry, fear, or a preoccupied state of mind for other reasons.

There is voluntary and involuntary attention. The former may be given because of the desire for praise if attention results in knowledge and work pleasing to the teacher. Or it may be because of a need for the information. A traveler asks directions of a stranger, and listens carefully to the answer.

Involuntary attention is the result of interest. It requires no effort of will to give heed to pleasing matters.

Perhaps the Master was not much concerned with this subject because his personality and his methods naturally enabled him to have a hearing at all times. But it becomes us who are not so gifted to learn the things he did and said and his means of approach, that we might have measurably satisfactory results.

It has been stated that there are three doorways of the soul by which attention may always be gained. They are: (1) Interest, (2) curiosity, and (3) appeals to the instinct of imitation.

There is a pedagogical law that says the learner must attend with interest to the truth or fact to be learned.

Jesus always had a point of contact and so interest was assured. Many were bound to him through gratitude for healing.[1] Such miracles opened the way for the Sermon on the Mount which followed.

On many occasions the point of contact was presented by a questioner. He went from the question to the lesson he desired to teach. The Gospels are full of accounts like this.

The occasion for teaching may have arisen as he talked to a group or partook of a meal. It may have been because of a problem put before him or a report of some recent happening or the critical thoughts of people. It may have been because people murmured at the waste of money when a

---
[1]Matt. 4:24.

woman anointed his head with expensive ointment. We cannot conceive of the Teacher's ever letting an opportunity go unheeded.

But we must not think of him as dependent upon such experiences, for he made occasions himself. We recall the blind man he healed, the man whom the Pharisees put out of the synagogue because he stood up for Jesus. When Jesus learned that they had cast him out, he sought him and taught him a helpful truth.[2]

Often the point of contact was by means of a story or a catchy saying. The Jews were all interested in the kingdom, so the Teacher was sure of attention when he used this subject. The parable of the sower, with which he began this parabolic method of teaching, had the advantage of being (1) a story and (2) a story on the interesting subject of the kingdom.

The Sermon on the Mount began with paradoxical sayings quite different from the usual expressions.

Jesus invited friendship. Modern teachers are copying his method of friendly association when they go on picnics or have banquets or go on hikes or play games with their pupils.

Sometimes, without speaking, the Master established the point of contact. When Peter had shown his weakness by denying his Lord, Jesus looked at him. This was all that Peter needed. He felt the rebuke, and in shame and contrition, "he went out and wept bitterly." (Luke 22:62.)

Jesus always had the interest of people. His fame went abroad and all men were eager to see and hear him. Some listened because of their interest in the things he said, and some because of their desire to catch him in mistakes and hinder his work.

---

[2]John 9:1-41.

He often added to this interest, before beginning to speak, by calling for attention. He made the call in such words as these: "Behold"; "Hear"; "Take heed"; "Verily, I say unto you"; "Hearken to me."

When about to visit certain communities "the Lord appointed seventy others, and sent them on ahead of him, two by two, into every town and place where he himself was about to come." (Luke 10:1.) Some modern evangelists adopt this method with marked success.

When he had their attention, he used it by an interesting beginning. This may have been a story or a catchy way of stating a truth or a reference to daily affairs in which his hearers were interested.

This interest was based on their past experience. He began with the familiar. We have devoted a chapter to the subject of apperception. It is well to say in passing that the use of apperception, associating the new with the old, is a big help in sustaining interest and holding attention for the teaching of great truths.

He sustained interest and, consequently, held attention by going rapidly to the matter in hand. The point of contact established and interest aroused, he went quickly from some lesser matter to a profound spiritual truth.

The lesson always developed under his handling. The human mind needs new things to be put before it, for very few people listen continuously with interest. Most minds are undisciplined and people are more likely to catch pointed expressions than grasp labored arguments. Not many teachers and preachers would feel flattered if they knew the good stopping places their hearers notice and would like them to discover.

The Master Teacher never let interest flag. With this gone, the teacher might as well stop unless he knows how to recover it.

Jesus was interesting, also, because he knew his subject thoroughly. He spoke from extensive knowledge. Then, too, he was living his lessons, and so he spoke from experience. He put his life into the message.

Appeal to curiosity was characteristic of some of the Master's teaching. He said of Nathanael, "Behold, an Israelite indeed, in whom is no guile!" And the man was curious to know how Jesus had known him.

Jesus used the curiosity of his disciples to teach the lesson of spiritual food. He said, "My food is to do the will of him who sent me, and to accomplish his work." (John 4:34.)

Zacchaeus was so filled with curiosity about Jesus that he climbed a tree to see him as he passed. And Jesus stopped beneath the tree and said, "Zacchaeus, make haste and come down; for I must stay at your house today." (Luke 19:5.)

The teacher who can arouse questions in the pupil's mind or who can present an interesting problem to be solved will be using this instinct of curiosity. We need to make our pupils hunger and thirst for instruction. Having aroused their mental and spiritual appetites, it will be a delight to fill their hungry minds and souls.

Jesus knew the value of an appeal to the instinct of imitation. He was continually setting the right example and asking his disciples to do as he did. He was the Good Shepherd who led the way. When he had illustrated humility by washing the disciples' feet, he said, "Do you know what I have done to you? You call me Teacher and Lord; and you are right, for so I am. If I then, your Lord and Teacher, have washed your feet, you also ought to wash one another's feet. For I have given you an example, that you also should do as I have done to you." (John 13:12-15.) And again, "If any man would come after me, let him deny himself and take up his cross and follow me." (Matt. 16:24.)

He in effect urged men to imitate God who "makes his sun rise on the evil and on the good, and sends rain on the just and on the unjust." (Matt. 5:45.) He exhorted, "You therefore, must be perfect, as your heavenly Father is perfect." (Matt. 5:48.) And so by imitation of the perfect, men grow more and more like the Master.

The vitality and enthusiasm of the teacher will have much to do with interest and attention. Jesus seems to have guarded his strength. He was always ready for the task and enthusiastic about his message. He even believed in man's future though he himself had been so shamefully ill-treated. He was always hopeful and so he filled his pupils with enthusiasm. We see this in the sacrificial zealous lives of the apostles and of many Christians throughout all the ages.

12.

His Use of Apperception

New knowledge depends upon the old. Apperception is simply the interpretation of the unknown by means of the known, or learning the new by beginning with the old. The process of assimilation by associating old objects with closely related new ideas is the process of apperception.

This applies to thoughts and ideas as well as to tangible objects, for in learning we must proceed from the known to the unknown. A familiar object helps us to understand an unfamiliar object or thought that is in some way related to it. And also, in thinking we cannot reason from what we do not know.

An illustration or two may be needed here. A Washington, D. C., pastor escorted a scrubwoman to Congressional Library and showed her the wonderful architecture and sculpture and the beauty of design and arrangement in this most beautiful building. She said nothing until they had left the building. Then, as she heaved a sigh, she said, "My, how much floor there is to scrub!"

A little child, raised in the country and accustomed to cows and goats and cats, was taken for the first time to a zoological garden. He saw animals of which he knew nothing and he called buffaloes "cows," tigers "kittens," and ibexes "goats."

As soon as the mind begins to function, it accumulates what we may call "images" or "perceptions" or "thoughts." The mind becomes familiar with certain objects, and a conception is formed of the objects in their relationships. Apperception begins when the mind interprets the new in terms of the old. It is not a mental result like the images with which we begin to get impressions early in life, but rather, apperception is a mental process.

Horne says, "To show the relation of apperception, as a process of interpreting new experiences according to old ones, to sensation and perception, it might be said that apperception is the mental assimilation of a sensation resulting in a perception."[1]

Jesus used apperception a great deal. His mental pictures, his objective illustrations, his parables, and his allegories all show how skilfully he proceeded from the known to the unknown.

The Samaritan woman at the well could think of nothing but the water in the well when Jesus first spoke of living water, but later in the conversation, the Teacher enabled her to rise to a conception of spiritual things.

Jesus talked with a ruler of the Jews, Nicodemus, about the new birth that was necessary before one could enter the kingdom of heaven. The learned man knew of natural birth, but he was unable to think his way from this knowledge to the spiritual idea. Then Jesus showed an understanding of

[1]From *Psychological Principles of Education,* by Herman Harrell Horne. Copyright, 1906. Used with the permission of The Macmillan Company.

apperception, though of course the term was not in use then. He said, "If I told you earthly things and you do not believe, how can you believe if I tell you heavenly things?" (John 3:12.)

One day a centurion besought the Master to heal his palsied servant. Jesus said, "I will come and heal him." But the centurion's faith was so implicit that he believed the Master could heal without even going into the presence of the sick. We call this centurion's faith an apperceptive condition for the use of Christ's power. It was the point of contact between the Healer and the centurion.

There were other times when the work of Jesus was hindered because of people's unbelief. The Pharisees and Sadducees of our Lord's day were so blind in their religious zeal that spiritual discernment was impossible. They could not see God in Christ. Their fathers had beheaded prophets and these men had not repented at the preaching of John the Baptist nor at the good news proclaimed by Jesus. They were "a disobedient and contrary people." (Rom. 10:21.) They could not apperceive. Indeed Jesus came near to stating the law of apperception when he said, "Seeing they do not see, and hearing they do not hear, nor do they understand." (Matt. 13:13.)

The Teacher's first parable was a clear illustration of this law. It was the parable of the sower. He named four kinds of soil, but the seed was the same. The harvest results from the combined response of soil and seed. "This central truth, applied to the Kingdom, means that it grows into fruitfulness by the Word of God, but that His Word is effective according to the spiritual apperception, and consequent responsiveness, which that Word finds in the hearts of men."[2] He

[2]From *The Jesus of Our Fathers,* by John Walter Good.

closed the parable with the words: "He who has ears, let him hear." (Matt. 13:9.)

In his later conversation with the disciples, Jesus gave as his reasons for using parables two facts: First, the disciples were spiritual and so were entitled to direct statement of the truth, but the others were not spiritual and so were denied this.

Spiritually minded as were the disciples, they were very slow in apperception of spiritual truth. The new ideas were unlike the old. Their old ideas were of legalism and of an earthly kingdom with a visible throne and a physical Monarch. Even on the day of his ascension they asked, "Lord, will you at this time restore the kingdom to Israel?" (Acts 1:6.) Never until they got his viewpoint were their relations with the Master perfected.

The teachings of Jesus were lost on many of his hearers. The Pharisees missed the point. The crowds were enthusiastic about him and yet many followed because they ate their fill of the loaves. (John 6:26.)

The tragedy that brought burning tears to his eyes was the knowledge that Jerusalem that killed the prophets and received him not would be destroyed because she knew not the time of her visitation.

Jesus longed for his people to apperceive him. But their thoughts were of the world. "He came to his own home, and his own people received him not." (John 1:11.)

We find the centurion at the cross getting a ray of understanding when out of the darkness he said, "Truly this was a Son of God!" (Matt. 27:54.)

Pilate asked Jesus, "Are you the King of the Jews?" (Matt. 27:11.) Matthew, Mark, and Luke each give Christ's answer, "You have said so." But John names a question that the Master put to Pilate, "Do you say this of your own accord, or did others say it to you about me?" (John 18:34.) Pilate's reply showed a lack of spiritual perception. His mind was barren of ideas of a spiritual kingdom. Jesus answered, "My kingship is not from the world." (John 18:36.) This helped Pilate to get at least one clear idea—the idea that Jesus claimed to be some sort of king, so he asked, "So you are a king?" (John 18:37.) In his affirmative answer, Jesus stated that to this end he was born and came into the world, "to bear witness to the truth." (John 18:37.) He added: "Every one who is of the truth hears my voice." (John 18:37.) In the language of our present discussion, he said, Every one who has apperceptive basis of truth that is necessary will recognize and respond to me as the Son of God and king of the world.

The greater our understanding, the greater will be our interest in things. He who has understanding eyes with which to see the most can get the most out of life. "For to him who has will more be given, and he will have abundance; but from him who has not, even what he has will be taken away." (Matt. 13:12.) This is the message of the parables of the pounds and of the talents, and it is a law of life. It is not from seeing with the natural eye, hearing with the natural ear, nor is it from cramming facts into the mind that real knowledge is gained. It is what we apperceive that really increases knowledge.

In the light of these facts, we know that many a person goes through the forms of spiritual life—giving money, attending worship, working at Christian tasks, participating in prayer, partaking of the Lord's Supper—and yet has not genuine spiritual knowledge. Again, many men intellectually rich are spiritually poor.

The feelings and the will play an important part in forming moral and religious ideas, and consequently in the ap-

99

perception of spiritual truth. It is vital, then, for the teacher of religion to apperceive the things of Jesus Christ and his kingdom.

In teaching we can teach only what the pupil's past knowledge has prepared him for. The Great Teacher was very careful about this. To modern teachers, then, is committed the task of knowing what their pupil's past has been, what his present is, his environment and his knowledge and thinking. Upon these we must build the spiritual structure patiently and lovingly.

This was the Master's advice to his disciples who declared they had grasped his meaning in parables. He said, "Therefore every scribe who has been trained for the kingdom of heaven is like a householder who brings out of his treasure what is new and what is old." (Matt. 13:52.)

He illustrated how to do this. He showed that as physical hunger was the forerunner of eating food, so with the spiritual hunger "Blessed are those who hunger and thirst for righteousness, for they shall be satisfied." (Matt. 5:6.)

They were with him constantly and saw his method of leading to apperception. And they learned the lesson. John showed an understanding when he wrote in his Gospel, "The light shines in the darkness, and the darkness has not overcome it." (John 1:5.)

The use Matthew and Luke made of apperception in the arrangements of the Gospels that bear their names forms a fascinating study. Matthew wrote for the Jewish people. Jews were familiar with the Old Testament Scriptures as well as with tradition. They had a lively hope for the coming of a king who would restore Israel's greatness.

Matthew began his Gospel with the genealogy of Jesus Christ, tracing it back to Abraham through David. This would be a strong point with Jews who knew that in Abraham's seed would all the nations of the earth be blessed, and who knew that the king would be in the line of David.

When the genealogy was given, Matthew next told of the wonderful birth of Jesus. Matthew began his record with the genealogy, for this was the most hopeful approach to this people, and then he added the truths necessary to teach of the spiritual and universal kingdom.

Luke was writing for Gentiles. They were religious but were not occupied with Old Testament prophecies. They had ideas of national deities and of sons of the gods.

How wisely, then, Luke first presented facts of the supernatural birth of Jesus Christ! And he presented him not simply as a son of God but the Son of God. He was different from the pagan conception, but they were prepared to understand this idea from the ones they held.

Then Luke gives the genealogy of Jesus Christ. He does not trace it simply to Abraham, but back further to the first man and to God himself—not to Abraham, the father of the Jewish people, but to Jehovah, the father of all nations of the earth.

Matthew and Luke each had the point of contact best suited for the minds of his readers. We see that they followed their Master's method in observing this law of apperceptive contact.

13.

His Use of Motivation

A motive is that which determines one's choice or will. It is what moves us to act or tend to act.

The task of the Christian teacher is to discover what motives are effective in securing right choices, choices that are in accord with Christian principles. Having made this discovery, the teacher's task is to nurture these motives in the lives of the pupils.

We have looked to Jesus for the statement of Christian principles, and we have found that he lives as he taught. Now we look to him for right motives in life, and we find ourselves discovering these in large measure as we learn the motives actuating him. He once said, "A disciple is not above his teacher, nor a servant above his master; it is enough for the disciple to be like his teacher, and the servant like his master." (Matt. 10:24-25.)

His motive was always one of unselfishness. He gave up ease, that he might take the good news to various places. To his disciples he said, "Let us go on to the next towns, that I may preach there also; for that is why I came out."

(Mark 1:38.) Luke quotes him in these words: "I must preach the good news of the kingdom of God to the other cities also; for I was sent for this purpose." (Luke 4:43.) During the wilderness temptations he could have satisfied his hunger by changing the stones into bread.

When fatigued from teaching and healing, he sought the necessary quiet and rest for himself and his disciples, "For many were coming and going, and they had no leisure even to eat." (Mark 6:31.) They went to a desert place. But "Now many saw them going, and knew them, and they ran there on foot from all the towns, and got there ahead of them." (Mark 6:33.) "Jesus had compassion on them, because they were like sheep without a shepherd; and he began to teach them many things." (Mark 6:34.)

He often made it clear that he sought to do the will of God. Even in his Gethsemane agony, he cried, "Father, if thou art willing, remove this cup from me; nevertheless not my will, but thine, be done." (Luke 22:42.) To the disciples who urged him to eat, he said, "My food is to do the will of him who sent me, and to accomplish his work." (John 4:34.)

He was moved by the spirit of love. He laid down his life in this noble spirit. He was always actuated by unselfish motives.

Jesus was more concerned about the motive than about the act. Long years before, the LORD had said to Samuel, "Man looks on the outward appearance, but the LORD looks on the heart." (1 Samuel 16:7.) Jesus made a similar statement: "God knows your hearts; for what is exalted among men is an abomination in the sight of God." (Luke 16:15.)

Men of his day, his followers and his enemies, were often actuated by wrong motives. In his effort to induce right

103

motives of conduct, the Teacher often contrasted the prevailing reason with the ideal.

One wrong spirit was insincerity. To overcome this he said, "Beware of practicing your piety before men in order to be seen by them; for then you will have no reward from your Father who is in heaven." (Matt. 6:1.) The spirit that would move people to seek praise of men annuls God's favor. True worship is impossible without sincerity. Jesus then contrasted insincerity in external forms of worship with genuine worship.

First, he spoke of almsgiving. Many hypocrites gave with great display. Trumpets would be blown by the recipients of their gifts, that passers-by on the streets might know of the gift. The gift had been for man's glory, not for God's. Jesus rebuked it.[1] Then he enjoined secrecy in almsgiving. By giving in this way the act would be sincere and the recipient would not be embarrassed.

Right giving is prompted by the right motive. It is sincere. It is not for praise. It is quite conceivable that one might present his gifts in public contributions with the same altruistic motive.

Next, the Master deals with the element of sincerity in prayer. "When you pray," said he, "you must not be like the hypocrites; for they love to stand and pray in the synagogues and at the street corners that they may be seen by men. Truly, I say to you, they have their reward." (Matt. 6:5.) This was insincerity. It was not real prayer, and all the reward they got was the hollow praise of men, the reputation of being devout. In contrast, Jesus desired his disciples to pray in order to commune with God.

---

[1]Matt. 6:2-4.

Prayer is never a public performance. That is, it is not for show.[2] Of course prayer can be genuine when among men. We are taught to "pray without ceasing." And in the early history of the church, the disciples went to a place where prayer was accustomed to be made. Jesus prayed in the presence of his disciples. His disciples, after his departure, prayed together and were the better prepared for the blessings of the first Pentecost that followed his ascension. Then, too, if the motive is right, one is unlikely to be guilty of "vain repetitions." He will know that God doesn't hear one for his much speaking.

Then the Master taught his disciples how to pray. He put first the things of God's interests in this world.

Hallowed be thy name.
Thy kingdom come,
Thy will be done.
These three petitions are characterized by the word "thy." The next four represent man's needs, and give prominence to "us" and "our."

Give us this day our daily bread,
And forgive us our debts,
    As we also have forgiven our debtors;
And lead us not into temptation,
    But deliver us from evil.

                    —Matt. 6:9-13.

Then the Master spoke of fasting. In his day, it was a much-abused custom. We find much insincerity accompanying it. Jesus taught, "When you fast, do not look dismal like the hypocrites, for they disfigure their faces that their fasting may be seen by men. Truly, I say to you, they have their reward." (Matt. 6:16.) Jesus would have

---

[2]Matt. 6:6.

105

his hearers know that such a motive was wrong. Fasting, like almsgiving and prayer, was a spiritual act. He taught them not to fast to make an impression on people.

Thus in all of his sayings the Master taught sincerity as the essential motive in worship.

Matthew records eight woes with which Jesus denounced hypocrites because their motives were ungodly.[3] In a general way these woes may be contrasted with the eight beatitudes in the Sermon on the Mount.

Did Jesus ever appeal to fear as a motive for right behavior? Yes, but it was by no means his primary appeal.

When all the higher appeals have failed, fear may have its place. This is the case with the scenes of the judgment, the references to weeping and gnashing of teeth, the references to the fire prepared for the devil and his angels, the story of the rich man in Hades, and the reference to the betrayer, "It would have been better for that man if he had not been born."[4] (Matt. 26:24.)

Often comparatively small tugs will tow several large schooners down the Mississippi River to the Gulf. After a while the sails will be unfurled, the ropes untied. The sails will be filled with wind and the boats go on their journey over the sea, leaving the tug behind. Fear may be the tug that starts some souls on the ocean of life, but soon the love of God will fill that life, and the soul will go on its journey leaving fear far behind.

There were other native reactions to which the Master appealed. We have shown in an earlier chapter, "His Use of Attention," that he appealed to curiosity. To Nathanael he said, "You will see heaven opened, and the angels of

[3]Matt., chapter 23.
[4]Some of his warnings are found in Matt. 11:21-24.

God ascending and descending upon the Son of man." (John 1:51.)

He appealed to sympathy by answering many calls of distress. It was just after his warnings to Bethsaida, Chorazin, and Capernaum, that he spoke these words of invitation and of sympathy: "Come to me, all who labor and are heavy-laden, and I will give you rest. Take my yoke upon you, and learn from me; for I am gentle and lowly in heart, and you will find rest for your souls. For my yoke is easy, and my burden is light." (Matt. 11:28-30.) He called for sympathy when he himself was in distress in Gethsemane: "My soul is very sorrowful, even to death; remain here, and watch with me." (Matt. 26:38.)

Many were the instincts to which he appealed, but the greatest of all was love. His disciples loved him and he urged them to love one another: "A new commandment I give to you, that you love one another; even as I have loved you, that you also love one another." (John 13:34.) "We love, because he first loved us." (1 John 4:19.)

As he himself was unselfish, actuated always by love for God and man, and submitting ever to the Father's will, we are not surprised to find him continually teaching men to act from the same motives. He made genuine love, unselfish love, the law of the kingdom.

Jesus taught lessons about reward and punishment. The golden text of the Bible states the reward of faith.[5]

The Master suggested to the Samaritan that he could give her "living water."

He spoke to his disciples about the reward of finding one's life in following him and in self-denial and bearing one's cross. The reward will be according to one's deeds. To

---

[5]John 3:16.

those who would seek first the kingdom of God, there would be added the necessities of life.

At the great judgment there will be rewards and punishments. If one builds foolishly, destruction will result; if wisely, he will withstand the storm.

Peter once said, "Lo, we have left everything and followed you. What then shall we have?" (Matt. 19:27.) And Jesus promised eternal life to those who followed him.

While Jesus taught the plain truth in regard to reward and punishment, he seems not to have used these as the great motives of life.[6]

Jesus endeavored to motivate conduct by means of altruistic ideals.

---

[6]In *The Ethics of the Dust* John Ruskin has stated what appears to be the function of rewards and punishments of the gospel. B. A. Hinsdale in *Jesus as a Teacher* has adapted the passage to read:

> The essential idea of real virtue is that of a vital human strength, which instinctively, constantly, and without motive, does what is right. You must train men to this habit, as you would the branch of a tree; and give them instincts and manners (or morals) of purity, justice, kindness, and courage. Once rightly trained, they act as they should, irrespectively of all motive, or fear of reward. It is the blackest sign of putresence in a national religion, when men speak as if it were the only safeguard of conduct; and assume that, but for the fear of being burned, or for the hope of being rewarded, everybody would pass their lives in lying, stealing, and murdering. I think quite one of the notablest historical events of this century (perhaps the very notablest) was the council of clergymen, horror-struck at the idea of any diminution in our dread of hell, at which the last of English clergymen whom one would have expected to see in such a function, rose as the devil's advocate to tell us how impossible it was we could get on without him. [Men] should be afraid of doing wrong, and of that only. . . . Otherwise, if they only don't do wrong for fear of being punished, they have done wrong in their hearts already. [God] never would be pleased with us if [our desire to please Him should be our first motive]. When a father sends his son out into the world —suppose an apprentice—fancy the boy's coming home at night, and saying, "Father, I could have robbed the till to-day, but I didn't, because I thought you wouldn't like it." Do you think the father would be particularly pleased? He would answer, would he not, if he were wise and good, "My boy, though you had no father, you must not rob tills"? And nothing is ever done so as really to please our Great Father, unless we would also have done it, though we had no Father to know of it. And how vain both [threatenings and rewards] with the Jews, and with all of us! But the fact is, that the threat and promise are simply statements of the Divine Law, and of its consequence. The fact is truly told you,—make what use you may of it; and as collateral warning, or encouragement, or comfort, the knowledge of future consequences may often be helpful to us; but helpful chiefly to the better state when we can act without reference to them. And there is no measuring the poisoned influence of that notion of future reward on the mind of Christian Europe in the early ages. Half the monastic system rose out of that, acting on the occult pride and ambition of good people (as the other half of it came out of their follies and misfortunes). There is always a considerable quantity of pride, to begin with, in what is called "giving ourself to God." As if we had ever belonged to anybody else.

Motives are classified as either egoistic or altruistic. It is questionable if any one, except Jesus, was ever entirely free from self-interest. None is perfect. Many are learning to change motives more and more from the seeking of good for self to the seeking of it for others. Unselfish motives are often manifested even by young children. Christian teachers have the opportunity of nurturing the purely altruistic choice in child and man. This is the very essence of Christianity.

Théodore Monod has sung of the change from egoism to altruism in the following poem:

Oh, the bitter shame and sorrow,
    That a time could ever be
When I let the Saviour's pity
Plead in vain, and proudly answered:
"All of self, and none of thee."

Yet he found me. I beheld him
    Bleeding on the accursed tree,
Heard him pray, "Forgive them, Father!"
And my wistful heart said faintly,
"Some of self, and some of thee."

Day by day His tender mercy,
    Healing, helping, full and free,
Sweet and strong, and ah! so patient,
Brought me lower, while I whispered:
"Less of self, and more of thee."

Higher than the highest heavens,
    Deeper than the deepest sea,
Lord, thy love at last hath conquered;
Grant me now my soul's desire—
"None of self, and all of thee!"

                              From the French.

The highest motives of life are essentially self-sacrificing. The true patriot, the devoted missionary, the faithful minister, the conscientious teacher, the worthy parent—all are moved by altruistic motives.

Early in life unselfish tendencies begin to appear. It is the duty of teachers of religion to nurture these instincts, to teach unselfishness and all else that is Christlike. Jesus taught that love is not self-seeking, and we know that if the motive is selfish, it is not prompted by love. Paul at a later date stated this fact in his love chapter: "Love does not insist on its own way." (1 Cor. 13:5.)

Jesus instilled right motives into his pupils by naming the ideals he wished them to seek. We have already outlined some of those to which he referred in the Sermon on the Mount in regard to sincerity in worship, in almsgiving, in prayer, in fasting in obedience to the will of God, in genuine love for friend and foe, and in continual forgiveness.

He showed that these motives of life were pleasing to the Father. He illustrated them by his own life. He set men to work doing the things that would free them from selfishness and develop the high ideals.

He ascended, leaving his disciples near Jerusalem for an experience that would start them forth as flaming evangels of the Gospel. He succeeded in changing them from men of prejudice, amounting to race hatred, to martyrs for the altruistic teachings of their Master.

It were folly to credit mere social influences with these results. These men had been with Jesus. They were men of God.

The mystical must not be left out as we seek to develop altruistic motives in others. Christians of all centuries have been conscious of an unseen power in their lives. Long before Jesus came, the prophets risked life and limb for this conviction that God was leading them. The writer of the Hebrew letter said, "God spoke of old to our fathers by the prophets; but in these last days he has spoken to us by a Son, whom he appointed the heir of all things, through whom also he created the world." (Heb. 1:1-2.) Jesus declared, "I do nothing on my own authority but speak thus as the Father taught me." "I always do what is pleasing to him." (John 8:28-29.) He wanted his disciples likewise to be in close touch with God.

The Christian motive includes social regeneration, but the center of the ideal is in Christ and not in society. "Ideals clearly stated, reinforced by example, put to the test in practice, linked with a system of religious beliefs, vitalized by the emotions, made supreme by mystical communion with the Infinite; this seems to have been the program of the Great Teacher and concerning its efficiency the history of the past two thousand years bears evidence."[7]

[7]From *The Pedagogy of Jesus in the Twilight of Today,* by Walter Albion Squires. Used by permission of Harper & Brothers, publishers.

14.

His Use of the Problem-
Project Method

"Like all great teachers, Jesus felt that real thinking begins with a problem."[1] According to Aristotle all knowledge starts in wonder. We are sure that Jesus wanted people to think right thoughts and secure accurate knowledge and live right lives. To this end, he used what teachers now choose to call the problem-project method.

A problem is a question proposed for solution. It may be a question concerned simply with knowledge, and hence be considered entirely mental. To solve it may have little effect on life.

Some problems are vital to the activities of life. Then there are some theoretical problems whose solution will have strong bearing on practical things. Belief in the deity of Jesus, faith in the promise of immortality, the solution of the problem of evil, and countless others may be considered theoretical, yet upon their solution depends man's behavior toward God and Jesus, and his actions will be influenced by his hope of a life after death.

---

[1]*What Did Jesus Teach?* by F. P. Graves.

Men have always had intellectual, emotional, and moral problems or needs. Problems of these kinds were brought to Jesus.

John the Baptist had an intellectual problem when he sent his disciples to Jesus with the question, "Are you he who is to come, or shall we look for another?" (Matt. 11:3.) Jesus helped John solve it by sending a message about the miracles he was working and of the fact that he was preaching the gospel to the poor. He helped John to think it out.

When Jesus and his disciples talked about his coming sufferings and his departure from them, their sorrow raised emotional problems.

Many moral problems were brought to him. Peter brought such a problem when he asked, "Lord, how often shall my brother sin against me, and I forgive him? As many as seven times?" (Matt 18:21.) The answer of Jesus made the number indefinite.

A moral problem was brought by a man in the Master's audience, when the man requested, "Teacher, bid my brother divide the inheritance with me." (Luke 12:13.) Jesus had just been talking about the time when his disciples would be brought before synagogues, rulers, and authorities and he had said, "Do not be anxious how or what you are to answer or what you are to say; for the Holy Spirit will teach you in that very hour what you ought to say." (Luke 12:11-12.) But one man, like many a church attendant of today, was not a good listener. His thoughts were on another subject. Probably he caught the words: "rulers and authorities," just spoken by the Teacher. He had a problem. No doubt he thought it simply an intellectual problem with a bearing on practical life, but it was deeper; it was moral. His chief interest was in property and it should have been higher. Jesus helped solve the deep problem. First, he asked, "Man, who made me a judge or a divider over you?" (Luke 12:14.) Then the Master used this problem as an occasion to teach the danger of covetousness, explaining that "a man's life does not consist in the abundance of his possessions." (Luke 12:15.) Then he told the parable of the rich fool.

Every need of man brought its problem. Men and women put before Jesus needs for forgiveness of sins, for solution of various sorts of difficulties in relation to God and man, for physical healing, for mental healing, for instruction in prayer, and for feeding of body, mind, and soul.

The people were conscious of some of the problems; some were known only to the Master. Back of some question there often lay a great need; and Jesus met the unspoken need and helped toward the solution of the unasked question as well as toward the expressed need and the problem that was stated.

Jesus would call attention to problems of which men were not thinking. This was doubtless true of much he said in the Sermon on the Mount.

Teachers who have used this method have found it most helpful. By presenting a problem in the very beginning of the lesson, they get attention and quicken interest. They enlist the mental activity of the pupils whose curiosity quickens the eagerness for an answer to the problem.

So little is this method of the Master used that its very use causes surprise. Henry Ward Beecher once advised young preachers to "cultivate the surprise power." Jesus seems to have adopted continually the plan of using a problem with the surprise element associated with it.

The Master did not give the answer to all problems nor did he deal with many of the matters that require solution. His message was a message of life, not of theories and facts of art, politics, science, philosophy, and business affairs. He did lay down principles, however, that enable men to solve all problems of right and wrong relation between men and between nations, as well as man's duty to God.

Jesus often used the project method in looking toward the solution of problems. A project is something to do. The thing to do may be intellectual, that is, something to work out mentally; or it may be a task for the hand, that is, some kind of physical activity such as handwork, blackboard or notebook work.

Recently a group of young people completed a project on Africa. They learned facts about the country, made maps of Africa and a model of a mission station on the Congo, built a model of the Bolenge Church, and a splendid copy of the steamship "Oregon" used by the missionaries.

Now the same group is busy on a Palestine project. A map of Palestine has been drawn. A large drawing of Solomon's temple has been prepared. A splendid relief map of Palestine, made of paper pulp, is a part of the project. Posters show birds, flowers, and animals of Palestine. Talks have been made on information obtained.

The project is purposeful activity. We know that one of the principles underlying teaching is the principle of self-activity. We must remember that a project involves mental as well as physical activity. In writing about the developing method we discussed this sufficiently. Certainly the Master Teacher devoted much time to arousing and guiding and enriching thought. But he went further than this. He assigned tasks to people.

Once he called the twelve to him and sent them out to do the things they had seen him do. They were to "Heal the sick, raise the dead, cleanse lepers, cast out demons." (Matt. 10:8.) They were inexperienced; they must learn.

115

But they went out to the difficult task and their success proved a great satisfaction and strengthened their faith.

At another time he sent seventy disciples on a similar project. When these messengers had finished their task, they came back filled with enthusiasm. Luke writes: "The seventy returned with joy, saying, 'Lord, even the demons are subject to us in your name!'" (Luke 10:17.) Of course they exulted in these new powers. Jesus knew how to teach them. He would not have men and women be as sponges. His pupils were not absorbers, but discoverers.

The mind and the hand, and the spiritual and the physical, are more closely related than men once knew. Work with the hands develops physical strength; this we all know. Work with the hands develops mental and moral strength; this we are beginning to learn. Work with the hands helps us conquer spiritual forces; this we are just learning from the Master. The hand of an intelligent man suggests intelligence in its movements.

He that would be great spiritually must serve. He who set the example of perfect spirituality worked for humanity with his hands and his whole physical, as well as mental and moral, being. In the words of Jesus, "The Son of man came not to be served but to serve, and to give his life as a ransom for many." (Matt. 20:28.) It was he who said, "Whoever would be first among you must be your slave." (Matt. 20:27.)

In his appeal to men through the intellect, he talked of sowing and reaping. In his appeal through activity, he set the example of projects of helpfulness, and he required it of others.

Almost at random we quote some of his words as he assigned projects that were to result in healing, or gaining of knowledge, or acquiring character, or learning the joy of helpfulness: "Follow me, and I will make you fishers of men." (Matt. 4:19.) "Sell what you possess and give to the poor, and you will have treasure in heaven; and come, follow me." (Matt. 19:21.) "If any one serves me, he must follow me." (John 12:26.) "Go and tell my brethren." (Matt. 28:10.) "Go therefore." (Matt. 28:19.) "Go and proclaim the kingdom of God." (Luke 9:60.) "Stretch out your hand." (Matt. 12:13.) "If any man would come after me, let him deny himself and take up his cross and follow me." (Mark 8:34.) "Zacchaeus, make haste and come down." (Luke 19:5.) "Feed my lambs." (John 21:15.) "Rise, take up your bed and go home." (Matt. 9:6.) "Jesus sent two disciples." (Matt. 21:1.)

Jesus knew that action was necessary. He knew there was "no permanent impression without definite expression."

Jesus used activity, then, as a part of the learning process.

Sometimes he used it early in the lesson. He began his conversation with the Samaritan woman at the well with a request of her to give him water.

Sometimes he used expressional activity later. He finished his Sermon on the Mount with words of warning in regard to the doing of things he had been teaching.

However, he did not always put a call for activity at the beginning or at the end of a series of lessons. He used it as a part of the learning process and he used it wherever it would be most effective. Jesus knew that people learn by doing.

We have found that he used the problem-project method at times when about to begin a lesson. For example, before he told the parable of the two sons, he raised the problem by asking, "What do you think?" (Matt. 21:27.) When a lawyer asked, "What shall I do to inherit eternal life?" Jesus started him on the mental project by asking in reply,

117

"What is written in the law? How do you read?" (Luke 10:25-26.) He told the parable of the lost sheep, partly as a question with a problem in mind. "What man of you, having a hundred sheep, if he has lost one of them, does not leave the ninety-nine in the wilderness, and go after the one which is lost, until he find it?" (Luke 15:4.)

There were other occasions on which the Teacher stated problems for his pupils to solve. When a blind man would see, Jesus gave him a project, "Go, wash in the pool of Siloam." The man "went and washed and came back seeing." (John 9:7.)

How many times projects have resulted in this way! The disciples went out to heal the sick and give sight to the blind. They served others even while getting the lesson Jesus wanted them to learn by this project. Their experiences were revealing. Like the blind man, they "came seeing."

Jesus gave a sick man a project: "Rise, take up your pallet, and walk." (John 5:8.)

When he said to his enemies, "Show me a coin. Whose likeness and inscription has it?" (Luke 20:24), he was assigning a project.

And all these projects accomplished a great purpose. We learn by doing. This is the principle Jesus deals with in the words, "If any man's will is to do his will, he shall know whether the teaching is from God or whether I am speaking on my own authority." (John 7:17.)

Thought leads to action. It was a part of his plan to arouse thought that prepared for action. Action also stimulates thought. Quite often it is important to express in action the thought we have, that this expression may deepen the thought with which we began. "Without doubt, when

Jesus made people think, they often acted better; also when he made them act, they thought better."[2]

Herbert Spencer once said, "The child should be taught as little as possible, and induced to discover as much as possible." No doubt Jesus would have agreed with this statement and have extended it to include adults as well.

We must not miss the purpose of the problem-project method. Right actions are the goal. But these right actions are to have back of them right thinking and right attitudes, with proper emotional responses. "Actions were to be changed by changing the inner nature, rather than the inner nature changed by changing the actions."[3]

It is quite conceivable that men will sometimes do right things from motives lower than the best. Some will obey the law of the land—a thing that should be done—but will do so because they fear being fined or imprisoned. Some will obey a command of Jesus Christ or follow a right custom of the church—a thing that all should do—but they may be doing it to win favor with certain persons or to have a social standing or to get a reputation for being religious. The problem-project method and other methods of Jesus were to establish high ideals above all else. With such ideals, Christian action will result. The adequate expression of Christian impressions will be genuine Christian activity.

The program of Jesus prepared his disciples for action. First, his teaching was preparatory. They did not go out on their mission at once. It took time to train. And when they went out on special tasks, they soon returned to the Teacher.

The ministerial student of our time must go out and preach even while still in college or seminary. Were he to

---

[2]Horne, *op. cit.*
[3]Squires, *op. cit.*

119

go out permanently and untrained except in the university of "hard knocks," he would be less prepared for his task.

The skill with which the Master taught during his few years of public ministry suggests careful preparation for the task during the years preceding.

The apostles needed his instruction and the projects he assigned, and after his departure they needed the Comforter. But when they finally launched forth, they manifested amazing activity.

The Master's teaching made workers. He made action and service the test of loyalty to him. "Thus you will know them by their fruits." (Matt. 7:20.) "Not every one who says to me, 'Lord, Lord,' shall enter the kingdom of heaven, but he who does the will of my Father who is in heaven." (Matt. 7:21.) "My mother and my brothers are those who hear the word of God and do it." (Luke 8:21.) "If you know these things, blessed are you if you do them." (John 13:17.) "You are my friends if you do what I command you." (John 15:14.) In his vivid description of the judgment, Jesus pictures the reward of those whose service had been right and the punishment of the inactive.

15.

His Use of Suggestion

Suggestion is mental and is one of the best educational processes. The idea suggested must be related to something already known in the mind and must appeal to some instinct or developed interest. It must be positive rather than negative. Furthermore, it must be addresssed to some active mental process through the will. With it must be associated a sufficiently strong incentive.

Jesus consciously used suggestion. He used it first by allusion. Many a time the Master suggested the right course by alluding to some who had done the right, or he suggested the avoidance of wrong by allusion to some whose wrongs were apparent.

Suggestion is most effective when indirect. Direct teaching is likely to be simply telling the pupil, and this is poor teaching. But the indirect method stimulates the mind to activity in search of truth.

Probably literature contains no better example of indirect teaching than the one recorded by Luke in which Jesus teaches neighborliness by means of the parable of the good Samaritan.[1]

Another splendid example is recorded by John.[2] The scribes and Pharisees took an adulterous woman to Jesus. They reminded him of Moses' command to stone such a person. Then they asked, "What do you say about her?" At first he was silent as he wrote with his finger on the ground. Then he spoke, "Let him who is without sin among you be the first to throw a stone at her." The suggestion was effective. They all went out one by one. He made them accuse themselves.

Not only should the suggestion be indirect but it should be positive. A negative suggestion tends to fill the mind with the very thing prohibited and consequently to lead to the doing of what is prohibited. But the positive suggestion puts the right act definitely before the mind.

It is generally poor psychology to forbid evil, but it is always wise to suggest the good.

The teachings of Jesus were usually positive. In the chapter on his use of declaratory didactic discourse, we referred to the negative form in which other religions had put the golden rule and to the positive language Jesus used in stating it.

There are other contrasts. The Ten Commandments are mostly negative. Jesus named eight beatitudes, all of them positive. The old law said, "You shall love your neighbor, and hate your enemy," but Jesus said, "Love your enemies and pray for those who persecute you."

Suggestion is often effective when put in the form of a question. This was the Master's use of the questions: "Do you not yet perceive? Do you not remember the five loaves

[1]Luke 10:29-37.
[2]John 8:3-11.

122

of the five thousand, and how many baskets you gathered? Or the seven loaves of the four thousand, and how many baskets you gathered? How is it that you fail to perceive that I did not speak about bread?" (Matt. 16:9-11.)

Illustrations are an effective means of suggestion. We have found how continuously the Teacher used apt illustrations, and that they were always perfect in form and wording. We now add that they were flawless in suggestion.

Jesus used suggestive words or artificial language in his indirect method of suggestion. His use of "Father," "many mansions," "house," "resurrection," "life," "house upon a rock," "house upon the sand," "if a blind man leads a blind man, both will fall into a pit," "you offspring of vipers! how can you speak good, when you are evil? For out of the abundance of the heart the mouth speaks"—all are suggestive words or suggestive figurative expressions.

The Master used suggestion is performing miracles of healing. To a sick man he suggested health: "Rise, take up your bed and go home." To blind Bartimaeus he said, " 'Go your way; your faith has made you well.' And immediately he received his sight and followed him on the way." (Mark 10:52.) A deaf mute was brought to him. Jesus took the man away from the multitude and before healing him used suggestion, for he "put his fingers into his ears, and he spat and touched his tongue; and looking up to heaven, he sighed, and said to him, 'Ephphatha,' that is, 'Be opened.' And his ears were opened, his tongue released, and he spoke plainly." (Mark 7:33-35.) Before restoring sight to another blind man, Jesus "spat on the ground and made clay of the spittle and anointed the man's eyes with the clay, saying to him, 'Go, wash in the pool of Siloam.' " (John 9:6-7.)

Jesus used suggestion in his miracles over nature. He was asleep in the stern of the boat during a storm. The disciples were frightened. "They awoke him and said to him 'Teacher, do you not care if we perish?' And he awoke and rebuked the wind, and said to the sea, 'Peace! Be still!' And the wind ceased, and there was a great calm." (Mark 4:38-40.) His benevolent action was a suggestion that he did care for their welfare.

The Teacher used suggestion for mental healing. A poor distracted father brought his epileptic boy to Jesus. The disciples had been unable to help and now the father pleads, "If you can do anything, have pity on us and help us." Before helping, Jesus must test and strengthen the father's faith. "And Jesus said to him, 'If you can! All things are possible to him who believes.' " Then in faith the father said, "I believe; help my unbelief!" (Mark 9:22-24.) And Jesus healed the boy!

The mission of Jesus was higher than the healing of body and mind. He had a message for the soul, and so from his miracles in these other regards came the spiritual messages.

Even when not performing miracles, he accompanied his teachings with appropriate actions. One time it would be to take a child in his arms. On another occasion "he rose from supper, laid aside his garments, and girded himself with a towel." When "they brought him all the sick, those afflicted with various diseases and pains, demoniacs, epileptics, and paralytics, and he healed them" (Matt. 4:24), he taught beautiful lessons of mercy and service as expressions of love. By his insistence on baptism at the hands of John, he taught obedience to God. When he cleansed the temple, his action was the suggestion that the house of God was a place of worship. It was by the suggestiveness of action that he gave the disciples of John the Baptist an object lesson to take to their leader.

His life was a continual suggestion of the influence of personality. It has always been true that people react to their surroundings unless they actively resist this tendency. Mind affects mind, character affects character. In his attitude toward life in all its relations and toward the Giver of life, the Teacher was continually suggesting right attitudes.

This beautiful strong Personality is alive today with his suggestions to all men. By the suggestion of his methods, teachers are learning true pedagogy; by the suggestion of his life, Christians are learning to be true to mankind; and by the suggestion of his ministry of helpfulness and sympathy and love for all mankind, the nations are beginning to learn true brotherhood.

16.

His Use of Habit
and Repetition

Repetition has much to do with habit formation.

The importance of directing life so as to form habits is
stressed by Horne. He says, "First, as teachers we must
think of the whole of education as a process of habit formation."[1]

Man has always had the tendency to routine and habit.
This condition is true of mental and spiritual habits as well
as of physical, and repetition tends to fix a habit permanently.

Habits of right living and thinking become strengthened
when the same right thing is repeated time after time. One's
capacity to serve and love is increased by the repeated use
of the power.

Unless we have moral and religious habits, we cannot
have moral and religious character. Without them there
could be no uniformity of faith and practice, and without
this there could be no co-operation.

_____

[1]*Op. cit.*

It is unfortunately true, though, that habits of religious procedure may become so fixed that religion becomes lifeless. It degenerates into forms and ceremonies. With many Jews the offering of sacrifices, paying of tithes, and the observing of sabbaths, new moons, and feasts, with the accompanying prayers and spreading forth of hands and ceremonial washings, took the place of justice, mercy, and walking humbly before God.

We know that Jesus had habits, inevitably so, for he took upon himself the form of man—and was, therefore, subject to all the trials, temptations, and habits of men. In childhood he formed habits of obedience to God and to Mary and Joseph, else he could not have increased in favor with God and man. He formed habits of regular attendance at the synagogue worship each sabbath. We read, "He came to Nazareth, where he had been brought up: and he went to the synagogue, as his custom was, on the sabbath day. And he stood up to read." (Luke 4:16.)

He formed habits of prayer. He habitually spoke in parables after the early part of his ministry. His custom was to do continually the things he taught others to do. His life was one of habitual devotion and loyalty to God and service to man.

But the Master was very anxious for religion to be genuine. He would have it the response of the heart rather than the system of a machine. Though giving two ordinances, baptism and the Lord's Supper, his chief stress was on a good life. He sought to develop faith and love. He stressed faith, obedience, and love as matters for each individual. Religion was not a national or even a family affair alone. It must involve vitally the individuals who make up the nation or family.

Jesus found it difficult to unmake the bad habits of his pupils, established for so many years. One method by which he sought to accomplish his aim was that of frequent repetition. He used the same or similar expressions, illustrations, or thoughts in many of his lessons. He had no horror of repetition. He realized that learning is slow. Teachers and preachers of every age have learned to repeat.

Repetition was necessary, and still is necessary, to aid the understanding or the memory or to prick the conscience.

One of the thoughts Jesus repeated time after time was that of his coming sufferings. He began this instruction shortly after his conversation with the twelve disciples at Caesarea Philippi. Matthew states it thus: "From that time Jesus began to show his disciples that he must go to Jerusalem and suffer many things from the elders and chief priests and scribes, and be killed, and on the third day be raised." (Matt. 16:21.) This was such a shock that Peter rebuked him. Time after time from then until his death, Jesus made reference to this event. In spite of the frequent repetition, even at the last when Jesus instituted the Lord's Supper with the little group of apostles, they could not grasp the idea. Yet he said of the bread, "This is my body," and of the cup, "This is my blood of the covenant, which is poured out for many for the forgiveness of sins." (Matt. 26:26, 28.)

He repeated instructions in regard to faith. He asked for faith when about to heal. He urged faith in God and in God's Son. He felt sorrowful when people manifested weak faith and said, "Why are you afraid, O men of little faith?" (Matt. 8:26.) "Where is your faith?" (Luke 8:25.) "Why are you afraid? Have you no faith?" (Mark 4:40.) He often taught faith in prayer. When he found exceptional faith, he commended it. He said of a centurion, "Not even in Israel have I found such faith." (Luke 7:9.) To a Canaanite woman, he said, "O woman, great is your faith!" (Matt. 15:28.)

His instructions about prayer were given on many occasions. He talked of it in the Sermon on the Mount, and at the time taught his disciples how to pray. Again, he contrasted the prayers of the Pharisee and publican.[2] He told the parables of the unjust judge[3] and the neighbor asking at midnight for bread,[4] to teach about prayer. He urged his disciples to pray.

Love was a hard lesson to learn. He said, "A new commandment I give to you, that you love one another; even as I have loved you, that you also love one another." (John 13:34.) Repeatedly he stressed the importance of the disciples loving each other.

He also taught them to love their enemies. This lesson was hard to learn but the Master kept on teaching it and showing how to do it.

His parables of the kingdom were many. It was a big subject but hard to understand because of the kind of kingdom the Jews were expecting.

Study of a concordance will show how often Jesus repeated his lessons about the Father, the Son's relationship to the Father, the Holy Spirit, the kingdom of God, the sufferings of Jesus, his second coming, hypocrisy, spiritual life, spiritual death, the resurrection of the dead, promises, faith, repentance, baptism, regeneration, works, love, forgiveness, will of God, faithfulness, watchfulness, steadfastness, patience, worldliness, judging, prayer, the law, joy, the Word, and other subjects. The Teacher is showing us that a lesson should be repeated until it has been learned.

[2]Luke 18:9-14.
[3]Luke 18:1-8.
[4]Luke 11:5-13.

17.

His Use of Analysis and Synthesis

Analysis is the separation of anything into its constituent parts. It may be used with the mental as well as the physical. In analysis we begin with the general and descend to the particulars.

Synthesis is the process of reasoning from the parts to the whole, or from particular cases to general cases.

To understand nature, we may proceed from causes to their effects. This is analytic. Or we may proceed from the effects to their causes. This is the synthetic method.

Jesus taught by both methods and so his way of teaching has been termed the analytic-synthetic method.

He taught much about the kingdom as a whole. The first sentence with which he began the Sermon on the Mount was a beatitude in regard to the kingdom. We see the analytic method from the beginning as he proceeds to speak of the qualities necessary for membership, its laws, and its territory. Then by synthesis, with the parts clearly defined, he made it possible for the kingdom as a whole to be comprehended.

We will find it profitable here to see his use of the analytic-synthetic method in regard to the kingdom he came to establish.

Jesus found the minds of Jews filled with the idea of a kingdom, but their conception was all wrong. However, beginning with this general interest in a promised and expected kingdom, he proceeded to talk a great deal about it. He gave no definition of it as a dictionary would define a word, but he proceeded by the analytic-synthetic method to help people see this kingdom in imagination.

Shortly after his baptism and season of wilderness temptation, he went into Galilee "preaching the gospel of God, and saying, 'The time is fulfilled, and the kingdom of God is at hand; repent and believe in the gospel.'" (Mark 1:14-15.)

He made his own announcement after the manner of his cousin John who had called upon the people to "Repent, for the kingdom of heaven is at hand." (Matt. 3:2.)

Later he selected twelve men, and these also he sent out to "preach the kingdom of God." (Luke 9:2.)

Again, he sent seventy, and told them to preach, " 'The kingdom of God has come near to you.'" (Luke 10:9.)

He told who could become citizens of the kingdom. He explained that a birth was necessary: " 'Unless one is born anew, he cannot see the kingdom of God.' 'Unless one is born of water and the Spirit, he cannot enter the kingdom of God. That which is born of the flesh is flesh, and that which is born of the Spirit is spirit.'" (John 3:3, 5-6.) This was difficult to understand when minds were full of ideas of a temporal, visible kingdom. A new viewpoint was needed—a new life, a pure heart, a hungering and thirsting after righteousness. This kingdom was to regenerate the life.

131

The Master extolled virtues of citizens of the kingdom of God to citizens of worldly kingdoms. They were to be as salt, or as light shining before men.

The Master discussed laws of the kingdom he was proclaiming. The supreme law is love. He spoke of laws that relate to man in his dealing with man. "You shall love your neighbor as yourself." (Matt. 19:19.) "You shall not kill." (Matt. 5:21.) He spoke of the sacredness of life.

He talked of social purity: " 'Have you not read that he who made them from the beginning made them male and female, and said, "For this reason a man shall leave his father and mother and be joined to his wife, and the two shall become one? So they are no longer two but one. What therefore God has joined together, let no man put asunder." ' " (Matt. 19:4-6.)[1]

He taught truthfulness with the need of no oath to strengthen it.[2] He taught not to render evil for evil but to do the opposite.[3] He often talked of the universal love that governed the hearts of the citizens of this heavenly kingdom.

Worship is important among citizens of the kingdom of God. He taught sincerity and genuineness for all worshipers. He spoke of it in regard to almsgiving, prayer, and fasting.[4]

He taught complete trust in and love for God and his Son.[5] He named laws of right living that involved a right attitude toward people, and a proper fitness for service to others.[6] He referred to a law of wealth.[7] Again he referred to prayer, and he pronounced the golden rule.[8] This

---

[1]See also Matt. 5:27-32.
[2]Matt. 5:33-37.
[3]Matt. 5:38-42.
[4]Matt. 6:1-18.
[5]Matt. 6:19-34.
[6]Matt. 7:1-5; Luke 6:37-42.
[7]Matt. 7:6.
[8]Matt. 7:7-12.

must be the spirit of all who pray acceptably. He named the law of faithful effort.[9]

There will of necessity be leaders in the kingdom. These are to be tested by their fruits.[10] Discipleship in the kingdom is tested also,[11] for it is because of obedience and genuineness of motive that one is acceptable.

Every one may qualify for membership in the kingdom. To those of his own race that received him, Jesus "gave power to become children of God." (John 1:12.) But he also included people from every nation under the sun, for he foretold that "many will come from east and west and sit at table with Abraham, Isaac, and Jacob in the kingdom of heaven." (Matt. 8:11.)

The kingdom was to grow. Its sway was to be everywhere as years before Isaiah had prophesied of the universal reign of the LORD:

It shall come to pass in the latter days
    that the mountain of the house of the LORD
shall be established as the highest of the mountains,
    and shall be raised above the hills;
and all the nations shall flow to it,
    and many peoples shall come, and say:
"Come, let us go up to the mountain of the LORD,
    to the house of the God of Jacob;
that he may teach us his ways
    and that we may walk in his paths."
For out of Zion shall go forth the law,
    and the word of the LORD from Jerusalem.
He shall judge between the nations,
    and shall decide for many peoples;

[9]Matt. 7:13-14.
[10]Matt. 7:15-20.
[11]Matt. 7:21-27.

133

and they shall beat their swords into plowshares,
  and their spears into pruning hooks;
nation shall not lift up sword against nation,
  neither shall they learn war any more.

          —Isaiah 2:2-4.

It was to grow in individual hearts: " 'The kingdom of God is in the midst of you.' " (Luke 17:21.) It was to grow by means of the family. Jesus declared that the family is of divine origin and that God wishes the family to remain a unit. He named but one reason for breaking this bond.[12]

Through the Christian family the possibility of the kingdom's growth is immense. When the family fails, the kingdom suffers terribly.

The church is closely identified with the kingdom. After Peter had confessed him as "the Christ, the Son of the Living God," Jesus said, "On this rock I will build my church." To Peter, probably as the spokesman of the apostles, the Master said, " 'I will give you the keys of the kingdom of heaven.' " (Matt. 16:19.) On the birthday of the church on Pentecost, the kingdom of heaven was established and "God has made him both Lord and Christ." (Acts 2:36.)

We have seen, in a measure in this study how faithfully the Teacher analyzed his kingdom. "The wide difference between his point of departure, the kingdom under the old economy, and the completion of his cosmic vision, the New Jerusalem conception of the kingdom represents the progress by intention and extension to be fully realized under the influence of the fuller revelation of his life and teachings. The former is the whole of apprehension; the latter, the whole of comprehension. This is the language of the analytic-synthetic method."[13]

---

[12]Matt. 19:9.
[13]Harrison Meredith Tipsword, *Pedagogics of Jesus* (Boston: Richard G. Badger, 1916), p. 102.

18.

His Use of Induction
and Deduction

Horne declares that induction and deduction are the two feet with which scientific progress has moved. As Jesus used both of these in teaching, it is important that we first understand the terms.

Induction is the process of reasoning from particular facts to general principles. By the inductive method, attention is given to particular facts or phenomena and general conclusions drawn from these. It is inferred that what is true of a number of cases will be true of others. From this come general principles applied to mankind as a race. The great Teacher laid much emphasis on the inductive method.

He continually stressed principles that were calculated to regenerate the individual, to bring to him a new understanding of God, a new sense of man's responsibility in life.

By changing the individual life he would thus change society and establish among men the principles of the kingdom. He did this when he taught: "Love your enemies, do good to those who hate you, bless those who curse you, pray for those who abuse you. Be merciful, even as your

Father is merciful." (Luke 6:27-28, 36.) To each individual came the command. Obedience is a personal matter. Forgiveness and salvation are individual. But if each lives according to the ideals of the kingdom as laid down by Jesus, then the general principles of the kingdom are the result.

Jesus also used deduction to a certain extent. In the process of deduction men reason from general principles to particular facts. Deduction is a conclusion from general premises: a fact from established data. It is the opposite of induction.

Deduction makes use of the discoveries of induction. For example: Paul asserted, "For whatever a man sows, that he will also reap." (Gal. 6:7.) Having declared this general principle, the accuracy of it may be proved by referring to many individuals whose experience shows this to be universally true.

Jesus used deduction in his statement of the Beatitudes. Back of all eight of these is the general principle that Jesus constantly illustrated and often talked about: the law of love, love to God and to man.

We hear him say, "Blessed are the poor in spirit. . . . Blessed are those who mourn. . . . Blessed are the meek. . . . Blessed are those who hunger and thirst for righteousness." With this general law of love in mind, for the Teacher stated it very clearly and forcefully in the same sermon, it is not difficult to understand these beatitudes in their individual application. If one proves his fitness for the kingdom of God by possessing the qualities named in these four beatitudes, qualities showing love for God, he may be tried by the four remaining beatitudes to see how his character stands in regard to the other of the great principles: "Blessed are the merciful. . . . Blessed are the pure in heart. . . . Blessed

are the peacemakers. . . . Blessed are those who are perse-
cuted for righteousness' sake."

The natural method of the human mind is to deal with
particular facts, then from these to draw general principles.
Thus having the general principles, it is natural for the human mind to deduce particulars from these. We first have
induction; then deduction.

Often the two methods are used together helpfully, as was
illustrated by the masterful way in which the Teacher used
them.

With those mentally prepared, the deductive method is
sometimes used first. The general laws are stated and application of the laws is made to new facts or information.

Tipsword says of Jesus: "He, himself, was the best data
for the establishment of the general principles which he came
to illume. But the effect of his teaching on the lives of
others is the surest deductive evidence of faithfulness to his
ideal of the more abundant life. The fruit those bear under
the influence of his teaching is the product of a healthy tree
which continues its yield of data in proof of his eternal life
principles. The happiness they realize in this right relation
of service is the strongest experimental application of the
same principles."[1]

---

[1]Tipsword, *op cit.*, p. 106.

19.

The Teacher's Last Lesson

Two discourses of the Master are recorded at some length. As we have sat together at the feet of this Great Teacher, we have listened with interest and delight and profit. But what a difference there is between the first of these—the Sermon on the Mount[1]—and the last, recorded by John.[2]

The first was a clear awakening call to duty. It was attention-arresting, thought-provoking, conscience-awakening. It was a startling announcement of the principles of the new order. It was a clear call to follow a new leadership away from mere form and ceremony to spiritual ideals and practical living. It was the introduction to the kingdom of heaven.

The second was entirely different. The Teacher and the little group of apostles had borne the heat of the day together and now the time of parting was at hand. Soon he must leave and another would lead them on. It was a time of sadness. "Let not your hearts be troubled." (John 14:1.)

[1]Matt., chapters 5, 6, 7.
[2]John, chapters 14, 15, 16, 17.

He talked lovingly of the Father and the Father's house where he was going to prepare a place for them. He promised to return to get them, but in the meantime he would not leave them without help. " 'But the Counselor, the Holy Spirit, whom the Father will send in my name, he will teach you all things, and bring to your remembrance all that I said to you.' " (John 14:26.)

The beloved Teacher talked on, telling how much the Father and Jesus and the disciples meant to each other. " 'I am the true vine, and my Father is the vinedresser. . . . Abide in me, and I in you. As the branch cannot bear fruit by itself, unless it abides in the vine, neither can you, unless you abide in me.' " (John 15:1, 4.) He reminded them of his love and urged that they love one another in the same way. He said: " 'It is to your advantage that I go away, for if I do not go away, the Counselor will not come to you; but if I go, I will send him to you.' " (John 16:7.)

And now as the night advanced and the Teacher was soon to depart, he talked to his Father about these pupils of his: " 'Father, the hour has come.' " (John 17:1.) He prayed to the holy Father: " 'Keep them in thy name which thou hast given me, that they may be one, even as we are one.' " (John 17:11.) He asked the Father to " 'keep them from the evil one.' " (John 17:15.)

Soon he looked beyond this little group to the many they would win to him. He prayed for these. He prayed for us. " 'I do not pray for these only, but also for those who are to believe in me through their word, that they may all be one; even as thou, Father, art in me, and I in thee, that they also may be in us, so that the world may believe that thou hast sent me.' " (John 17:20-21.)

A few minutes later the Teacher was betrayed into the hands of sinful men. A few more hours and he died, brokenhearted, upon the cross.

The passing years deepen the lessons taught by a beloved teacher and enrich life. Going down into death, into apparent defeat, dying with a broken heart, Jesus lives today more victoriously than ever in his life in the flesh on earth.

The disciples remembered the lessons he had taught by word and by life. They recalled his genuineness, his self-denial, his self-control, his sympathy, patience, compassion, forgiveness, his courage, his gentleness with the penitent and sternness with the hypocrite, his kindly consideration demonstrating his courtesy, his friendliness and willingness to be approached by all in need, showing his democratic spirit, his untiring activity in healing the sick and in teaching, showing his diligence.

They remembered that the Master was always trying to enrich life, to make it better and happier. His tests were the tests of character, rather than of knowledge or social standing or loyalty to forms with the spirit left out.

Best of all, they were continually recalling his perfect love, for there was never a love like his. It was an unequalled devotion to God and to humanity.

As the years passed, it was the delight of the apostles to talk about their Teacher and his lessons. Moreover, they learned to walk in his footsteps.

Today we are indebted to these pupils of his, and to some whom they taught, for his life story. It becomes us also to learn these lessons and teach with the greatest skill of which we are capable.

The disciple whom he loved said of the Teacher: "Having loved his own who were in the world, he loved them to the end." (John 13:1.) When all the methods of teaching have

140

been learned and used; when the teacher of today has done his best to teach as the Master taught and to live as the Master lived, loving with a love that gives itself to make lives better, then at the close of school, when good-by must be said, we will the better appreciate the parting scene of Jesus and the chosen few.

Not myself, but the truth that in life I have spoken,
　Not myself, but the seed that in life I have sown,
Shall pass on to ages—all about me forgotten,
　Save the truth I have spoken, the things I have done.

So let my living be—so be my dying;
　So let my name lie, unblazoned, unknown,
Unpraised and unmissed, I shall still be remembered—
　Yes, but remembered by what I have done.

—Horatius Bonar

Bibliography

Bagley, W. C. *The Educative Process.* The Macmillan Company, New York.

Barclay, Wade Crawford. *The Principles of Religious Teaching.* The Methodist Book Concern, New York.

Barton, Bruce. *The Man Nobody Knows.* The Bobbs-Merrill Company, Indianapolis.

Betts, G. H. *How to Teach Religion.* The Abingdon Press, New York.

Betts, G. H., and Hawthorne, M. O. *Method in Teaching Religion.* Abingdon Press, New York.

Brooks, Phillips. *The Influence of Jesus.* E. P. Dutton & Co., New York.

Bruce, Alexander Balmain. *The Parabolic Teaching of Christ.* A. C. Armstrong and Son, New York.

Chapman, J. C., and Counts, G. S. *Principles of Education.* Houghton Mifflin Co., Boston.

Coe, George A. *What Is Christian Education?* Charles Scribner's Sons, New York.

Colegrove, Chauncey P. *The Teacher and the School.* Charles Scribner's Sons, New York.

Crum, Mason. *The Project Method in Religious Education.* Cokesbury Press, Nashville, Tenn.

Darsie, Charles. *Adult Religious Teaching.* The Bethany Press, St. Louis, Mo.

Dods, Marcus. *The Parables of Our Lord as Recorded by St. Matthew.* Hodder and Stoughton, London.

Earhart, Lida B. *Types of Teaching.* Houghton Mifflin Co., Boston.

Eddy, Sherwood. *Facing the Crisis.* Association Press, New York.

Eggleston, Margaret W. *The Use of the Story in Religious Education.* Harper & Brothers, New York.

Farrar, Frederic W. *The Life of Christ* (Chapters 20 and 21). A. L. Burt, New York.

Fergusson, E. Morris. *Teaching Christianity.* Fleming H. Revell Co. New York.

Galloway, Thomas Walton. *The Use of Motives in Teaching Morals and Religion.* The Pilgrim Press, Boston.

Gilbert, George Holley. *The Student's Life of Jesus.* The Macmillan Co., New York.

Glover, T. R. *The Influence of Christ in the Ancient World.* Yale University Press, New Haven.

Graves, F. P. *What Did Jesus Teach?* (See chapters 2 and 3.) The Macmillan Co., New York.

Hall, G. Stanley. *Jesus, the Christ, in the Light of Psychology.* D. Appleton & Co., New York.

Hart, Joseph K. *Adult Education.* Thomas Y. Crowell Co., New York.

Hastings, James Ed. *Dictionary of Christ and the Gospels.* 2 vols. Charles Scribner's Sons, New York.

Hillis, Newell Dwight. *The Influence of Christ in Modern Life.* The Macmillan Co., New York.

Hinsdale, B. A. *Jesus as a Teacher.* The Christian Board of Publication, St. Louis.

Hites, Laird T. *Ways of Using the Discussion Method with Adult Classes.* The Christian Board of Publication, St. Louis.

Horne, Herman Harrell. *Jesus, the Master Teacher.* Association Press, New York.

Horne, Herman Harrell. *Story-Telling, Questioning, and Studying.* The Macmillan Co., New York.

143

Kilpatrick, William Heard. *Foundations of Method*. The Macmillan Co., New York.

Lawson, James Gilchrist. *Greatest Thoughts About Jesus Christ*. Harper & Bros., New York.

McKoy, Charles Francis. *The Art of Jesus as a Teacher*. The Judson Press, Philadelphia.

McMurry, Charles A. *Teaching by Projects*. The Macmillan Co., New York.

Myers, A. J. William. *Teaching Religion*. The Westminster Press, Philadelphia.

Roberts, Richard. *That One Face*. Association Press. New York.

Roberts, Seldon L. *Teaching in the Church School*. The Judson Press, Philadelphia.

St. John, Edward Porter. *Stories and Story-Telling in Moral and Religious Education*. The Pilgrim Press, Boston.

Shaver, E. L. *The Project Principle in Religious Education*. University of Chicago Press, Chicago.

Squires, Walter Albion. *The Pedagogy of Jesus in the Twilight of Today*. George H. Doran Co., New York.

Stevens, George Barker. *The Teaching of Jesus*. The Macmillan Co., New York.

Stevenson, J. A. *The Project Method of Teaching*. The Macmillan Co., New York.

Suter, John Wallace, Jr. *Creative Teaching*. The Macmillan Co., New York.

Tipsword, Harrison Meredith. *Pedagogics of Jesus*. Richard G. Badger, Boston.

Trench, Richard Chenevix. *Notes on the Parables of Our Lord*. Fleming H. Revell Co., New York.

Wayland, John W. *Christ as a Teacher*. The Stratford Co., Boston.

White, Goodrich C. *Teaching in the Sunday School*. Cokesbury Press, Nashville.

Winchester, Benjamin S. *The Church and Adult Education*. Harper & Bros., New York.